Disclaimer

This manual does not purport to offer legal advice or render legal opinions. By its nature, it is a general statement of the law. Therefore, it does not detail the law of product liability. Furthermore, product liability law is a matter of State law. While some generalities can be drawn, each State has its own body of law on this subject. Consequently, when legal counsel is necessary, an attorney should be consulted.

*Fundamentals
of Product Liability
Law
for Engineers*

Fundamentals of Product Liability Law for Engineers

Linda K. Enghagen, J.D.

Industrial Press Inc.

Library of Congress Cataloging-in-Publication Data

Enghagen, Linda K.
    Fundamentals of product liability law for engineers / Linda K
Enghagen.—1st ed.
        160 p. 15.6 × 23.5 cm.
    Includes bibliographical references and index.
    ISBN 0-8311-3039-3
        1. Products liability—United States. 2. Engineers—United States—
Handbooks, manuals, etc. I. Title.
    KF1296.E65   1992
    346.7303'8'02462—dc20   91-47855
    [347.3063802462]   CIP

First Edition

First Printing

Fundamentals of Product Liability Law for Engineers

Industrial Press Inc.
200 Madison Avenue
New York, New York 10016-4078

Composition by Paragraphics, Milford, Penn.
Printed and bound by Quinn Woodbine, Woodbine, N.J.

10   9   8   7   6   5   4   3   2

Contents

Preface

It is with some trepidation that I have undertaken to explain something about the rules of law and the legal system as they are encountered by those of you in the engineering profession. Lawyers are not high on the list of the most respected professionals these days, and I take that somewhat personally. After all, I have dedicated my professional life to the law—first as a student of law, second as a practicing attorney, and now as a teacher of the law. For me, the law is intellectually stimulating and, in its capacity to materially impact each of our individual and daily lives, truly awesome. The law, and the role of attorneys in the legal system, is also seriously misunderstood by many, if not most, nonlawyers. I lay the blame for that at the feet of lawyers, myself included, who have not insisted that the educational system school students in the legal system. One cannot understand the legal system or the legal profession if all one knows is the number of steps it takes for a bill to become a law in the legislative process and the appellate structure of the courts in the State and Federal court systems. Yet, in my experience, both as a student and now as a teacher of students, this is about the sum total of pre-college instruction in the legal system and the legal profession. Even at the college level, most students are not required to further study the law.

Consequently, I have two objectives in this book. First, it is my goal to provide engineers with a basic understanding of the rules of substantive law governing product liability litigation. Second, it is my goal to provide you with some insight into why lawyers go about practicing their profession in the way that they do. If a certain amount of defensiveness creeps into this, I apologize. I am proud to be a member of the legal profession. While I cannot defend or condone everything lawyers do or the ways in which they do them, I would also vigorously argue that most of what the majority of lawyers do is right and proper. The problem laypeople have in looking at what lawyers do rests in not understanding the rules and structure of litigation. It is not an undertaking for those who are weak of heart or who possess only a modicum of intestinal fortitude. In many cases, the stakes are high and the level of fighting is fierce. For attorneys, it is a game—yes, I said "a game"— of wits, strategy, and nerve. Who, if anyone, will blink first? It is also fun.

On a more philosophical note, I would like to address what I understand to be the basic underpinning of all law. In its most practical sense, the basic purpose underlying all law is the prevention of unnecessary harm. Whenever people live together, whether in the same household or in the same society, their daily interactions and physical proximity to one another give rise to the possibility of one person harming another. This is exacerbated when people are competing for what they perceive to be limited resources and opportunities. The law steps in to assist people in dealing with one another in a civilized manner. Now, it is certainly possible to question the wisdom of some laws—do they serve to prevent unnecessary harm, or is there a better way to accomplish that result? Nevertheless, I doubt many of us would prefer to go to the other extreme, where there is no authority such as law. So, I ask you to keep this thought in the back of your mind as you are reading these materials. Even if you do not agree with the law in its current manifestation or, more importantly, if you personally have had a bad experience with the legal system, step back for a moment and ask if the law, as it stands, serves the end of protecting people from unnecessary harm. I ask you to understand it in this context. I ask you to practice your profession in this context.

Linda K. Enghagen

Introduction

Product liability lawsuits generate more $1-million-plus verdicts than any other type of personal injury lawsuits except medical malpractice cases. As a matter of fact, as many as 29% of all product liability verdicts are returned with judgments of $1 million or more. Defendants lose 56% of all product liability lawsuits which go to trial. The injuries involved are of the most serious magnitude. Recent studies indicate that 24% of all product liability lawsuits involve death or an amputation; another 6% involve brain injuries. While liability is not predicated on the nature of the injury, it is easy to understand why plaintiffs and their attorneys pursue such claims. Statistically, the chances of prevailing are more than reasonable (from their perspective); and, given the gravity of the underlying injuries, the possibility of recovering a substantial verdict makes product liability claims attractive and remunerative. The claims are attractive and remunerative to plaintiffs and their lawyers, but not to the defendants who find themselves in the position of justifying and explaining past conduct and practices (or, in some cases, the failure to engage in certain conduct or the absence of certain practices).

The purpose of this manual is to provide engineers, managers, and other technical professionals with a basic background in product liability law. With this background, such professionals will be better prepared to work preventatively to avoid litigation, to develop documentation and procedures to defend against any litigation which does ensue, and to engage in damage control which will minimize the size of any verdicts or settlements which are unavoidable.

Toward these ends, the following areas will be addressed. First, the background of product liability law will be explored. What is the nature of civil lawsuits? Why is money the medium for resolution of these disputes? What happened to the doctrine of *caveat emptor*? Second, what is the basis of the types of claims which fall under the heading of product liability lawsuits? The differences between design defect, manufacturing defect, and misrepresentation cases will be examined. Third, what strategies are available for protection in product liability lawsuits? The use of proper inspection procedures, disclaimers, and warnings will be discussed. Fourth, what defenses are available to defendants in product liability lawsuits? Product misuse, contributory negligence, assumption of the risk, and comparative fault will be considered. Fifth, how does an attorney go about proving a case? Sixth, what types of evidentiary considerations arise in product liability considerations? And finally, what considerations lay beyond the basic requirements of the law? How do ethical concerns interrelate with questions of product safety?

Background of Product Liability Law

The development of product liability law is closely aligned with the evolution of the basic economic order from one which was agrarian based to one largely reliant on industry and specialization. In an agrarian-based economy, most individuals consumed what they produced. Bartering was the most commonly employed means of acquiring the few things which could not be produced. During this time, the legal system was a strong proponent of the theory that the greatest benefit would evolve from unfettered competition. A corollary to this theory was the doctrine of *caveat emptor* or "let the buyer beware." The belief underlying these principles was simply that those who produced inferior or defective products would be driven out of business because they would be unable to sell their wares. Buyers and sellers were on more or less equal footing, that is, they had equal bargaining power. Consequently, it is probably true that relatively little damage resulted from this approach when the economy was overwhelmingly agrarian in nature. However, as the development of machinery paved the way for industrialization and specialization, this changed. Buyers and sellers were not longer in relatively equal positions. Some sellers had virtual monopolies over certain types of goods. And, as products became more complex, buyers had less of an opportunity to make genuinely informed choices about product quality and safety. As a result of these changes, it became clear that a legal response was necessary. Two things occurred. One was that it became imperative that the law respond to this new economic order in which money was exchanged for products. Consequently, a body of law emerged to regulate such things as contracts and debtor/creditor relationships. A second development was the need for a body of law which could adequately respond to the injuries suffered by the employees and customers of the industrialists. Worker compensation laws and consumer protection laws, including product liability law, are current responses to this second development.

Modern product liability law is a twentieth century invention. Prior to 1916, an individual who was injured by a defective product had a claim only if that individual was also a party to the contract by which the product was acquired. For example, if a parent bought a defective toy which caused injury to a child, the child had no claim against the seller because the child did not buy the toy, the parent did. Obviously, this created unjust results. Modern product liability law addresses this inequity. It is designed to provide a legal remedy to a broad range of users of consumer products which cause personal injury or damage by virtue of some defective condition or misrepresentation caused by the designer, manufacturer, or seller of the product.

When a designer, manufacturer, or seller is found legally responsible in a product liability lawsuit, he or she has been found to have violated *civil law*. At first blush, this might appear to be an obviously elementary observation. However, the distinctions between civil and criminal lawsuits in the American legal system are far reaching, and frequently unknown or misunderstood. For example, consider the following illustration. Notice that while both civil and criminal law fall under the umbrella of constitutional law, the substantive and procedural law of civil lawsuits is separate and independent from the substantive and procedural law of criminal lawsuits.

CONSTITUTIONAL LAW

Civil Law	*Criminal Law*
SUBSTANTIVE LAW	SUBSTANTIVE LAW
PROCEDURAL LAW	PROCEDURAL LAW

While constitutional law is the standard by which the validity of all law is measured, the American legal system operates with two completely different subsystems for civil lawsuits and criminal lawsuits. Again, civil and criminal lawsuits each have their own rules of substantive law and procedural law. Substantive law is the body of law which spells out the peoples' duties and obligations. For example, it is a violation of criminal law to take the life of another unless that is done in self-defense. It is a violation of civil law to break a contract. Procedural law is the body of law which tells the parties to the lawsuit how to go about suing someone. For example, in criminal lawsuits, the lawsuit is started when the district attorney brings charges. In civil lawsuits, the lawsuit commences when the plaintiff's private attorney files a complaint with the appropriate court. In other words, procedural law establishes the method to be followed in suing someone. It tells the parties involved which pieces of paper must be filed when, and who must be notified of what, and how that must be done. Cases can be won or lost on either substantive or procedural law. To the victor's attorney, winning on a procedural issue is as satisfying as winning on the merits (i.e., substantive law). This is true for a number of reasons. First, as an advocate for a party's interests, a lawyer's job is to advance that client's interests through any legal means available. Second, lawyers are not inclined to view procedural law as a collection of "mere technicalities". Both substantive and procedural law are intended to promote justice through fair trials. This is central to a free and democratic society. And third, yes, a win is a win.

Broadly speaking, criminal law is classified as one type of public law, while civil law is classified as private law. Public law regulates the relationship between individuals and the government. (Other forms of public law are administrative law and constitutional law.) In contrast, private law regulates relationships between individuals. Both public and private law are vehicles for maintaining social order. Criminal law is a vehicle of social control in a literal sense. Its primary purpose is to provide for the safety of people and their property. Consequently, it allows for the most severe sanctions against those who transgress the rules through the imposition of such punishments as the death penalty (where allowed), imprisonment, and fines. The sanctions imposed for violations of civil law are far milder in comparison. Rather than deprive someone of life, liberty, or money (for the purpose of punishment), the primary sanction in civil lawsuits is an award of money computed to reflect the actual loss suffered by the aggrieved party. For example, if Sam breaches a contract with John, causing John to lose $5,000 which he cannot reasonably be expected to recoup, John would be awarded $5,000 (and no more) in a successful breach of contract lawsuit. Generally, when imposing a criminal fine, a judge is not concerned with the out-of-pocket losses of the victim, but with such things as the nature of the crime charged (e.g., misdemeanor or felony), whether or not violence or a threat of violence was used, and whether or not the criminal has a prior record.

Money is the primary medium of providing redress in civil lawsuits because the primary purpose is to compensate individuals for their actual losses which result from the unlawful conduct of another. The primary purpose of criminal lawsuits is to preserve the peace. Consequently, the sanctions imposed against criminals are designed to punish and deter individuals. (While some lip service continues to be paid to the notion that one of the purposes of the criminal justice system is to rehabilitate criminals, the Federal prison system officially abandoned such efforts in 1975 on the grounds that rehabilitation is impossible.)

One of the most striking differences between civil and criminal lawsuits regards the burden of proof. The burden of proof refers to the standard by which the evidence presented is evaluated to determine whether there is enough to find the defendant guilty (or legally responsible) for the offense in question. In criminal lawsuits, the burden of proof is *proof beyond a reasonable doubt*. That is, each element of the crime charged must be proven by proof beyond a reasonable doubt, which loosely translated means *proof to a moral certainty*. For example, murder is defined as the unlawful taking of the life of another. This is broken down into two elements: 1) the taking of the life of another, and 2) in an unlawful manner. Each element must be proven *to a moral certainty*. Consequently, if the prosecutor proves the defendant killed someone, but is unable to prove it was unlawful because the defendant introduces convincing evidence that he or she acted in self-defense, there is no murder—the defendant is innocent. Civil law-suits employ a materially less stringent standard. In most civil cases, the burden of proof is *proof by a preponderance of the evidence.* Roughly translated, this means *more likely than not.* Another way to think of it is that the party who presents the more convincing evidence wins. Obviously, it is far easier to meet the burden of proof in civil lawsuits than it is in criminal lawsuits. Product liabil-ity lawsuits are civil lawsuits and therefore use the evidentiary standard of *proof by a preponderance of the evidence.*

Theories of Liability

Introduction

There are six basic legal theories used in different types of product liability lawsuits. Negligence, strict liability, and misrepresentation are theories which are based in tort law. In addition, there are three theories which are derived from the law of contracts, specifically the law of sales contracts: express warranty, the implied warranty of merchantability, and the implied warranty of fitness for a particular purpose. To understand how a plaintiff's attorney determines which theory or theories to use in a particular case, it is helpful to understand the nature of the legal interests sought to be protected in tort and contract law.

Both tort and contract law are part of civil law and therefore are intended to define the legal relationships between private individuals. Contract law is the body of law designed to compel individuals to honor their promises. A contract is defined, in a very simple sense, as *a legally enforceable agreement.* Contract law attempts to compel individuals to perform their promises, and if that fails, it compels them to pay the innocent injured party for his or her losses which result from that breach. Tort law is not concerned with promises. It is designed to protect individuals from harm, both to their person and property, at the hands of someone who is acting in a manner deemed inappropriate to civilized society. It is not easy to provide a clear definition of a tort because the field of tort law is something of a catch-all category for violations of civil law which do not fit neatly into any other category. Nevertheless, a tort is typically defined as *a civil wrong, other than a breach of contract, which has harmed the person or property of another, for which the law allows a remedy in the form of an action for damages (i.e., money).* (Under limited circumstances, injunctive relief is ordered as well.)

From this general discussion, it follows that the theory or theories selected by a plaintiff's attorney in a particular product liability lawsuit depend on whether the alleged wrongdoing by the defendant was based on the defendant's failure to honor a promise (which may include failing to live up to a representation) or the failure of the defendant to satisfy the minimal standard of conduct required by the law to protect others from harm. A defendant will be found to have violated a promise if, for example, the delivered product does not meet stated specifications, or does not perform as stated in applicable warranties. A defendant will be found in violation of minimal standards of conduct if, for example, a product is unreasonably dangerous or is sold without appropriate warnings or operating instructions.

Broadly speaking, there are three types of product liability lawsuits based on what is alleged to be wrong with the product: design defect cases, manufacturing defect cases, and misrepresentation cases. Regardless of which theory is used, there are five basic facts a plaintiff seeks to prove in any product liability lawsuit: 1) the product was defective, 2) the defect existed at the time the product left the control of the defendant, 3) the defendant knew or should have known of the existence of the defect, 4) the defect caused harm to the plaintiff's person and/or property, and 5) feasible alternatives were available to the defendant to eliminate the risk caused by the defect or to bring it within a legally acceptable range. Note that the defect referred to here may be a defect in the product itself or a defect in representations concerning the product (e.g., warranties, instructions, or warnings). It is important to remember that the law *does not* require products to be perfectly and absolutely safe to be legally acceptable. It *does* require, however, that products be safe when their utility is balanced against the dangers inherent in their use, and against the cost and difficulty of making them safer. The following discussion will examine these three types of cases by evaluating how the six legal theories apply to the underlying problem(s) complained of.

Design Defect Cases

In many ways, design defect cases are the most difficult and potentially damaging (from the perspective of the defendant) type of product liability lawsuit. By definition, a design defect case alleges that a product is unsafe by virtue of the manner in which it was *supposed* to be manufactured. That is, the manufacturer followed the specifications in all respects, and the product still fails to meet legally, minimal acceptable standards of safety. In some cases, not only did the manufacturer follow specifications, but the design professionals followed existing manufacturing, governmental, and industry standards. Frequently, design defect cases are on the cutting edge of, if not product development, the law. This creates two major problems for the defendant in design defect cases. First, the defendant may find himself or herself with an entire line or warehouse full of a product which cannot be sold at all or only with costly modifications. Second, the defendant may be in a position where it was very difficult, if not impossible, to predict or anticipate the situation. While it is usually "safe" to rely on applicable manufacturing, governmental, and industry standards, this is not enough to insure against a loss in a design defect case. The allegation used as the basis of a challenge in these cases claims that all of these criteria are not enough. The standard sought to be used by the plaintiff is not industry or government based, it is based on a legal theory. Generally speaking, engineers and other design professionals have a legal duty to design a product in such a manner that it is safe for *any reasonably foreseeable use.* On its face, this sounds easy enough. But how does one determine what is reasonable and foreseeable? By the standard of someone with the life experience of a 50 year old or a 15 year old? Can reasonable people differ in their assessment of what is safe? The law provides three different legal theories which may apply to design defect cases depending on the specific facts of the underlying claim: negligence, strict liability, and the implied warranty of merchantability. The following will first discuss each of these three theories generally. Then, two design defect cases will be presented to illustrate how judges evaluate the legal theories when presented with a particular set of facts.

Negligence as a Product Liability Theory

In one of its classic definitions, *Black's Law Dictionary* defines negligence as: *the omission to do something which a reasonable [person] guided by those ordinary considerations which ordinarily regulate human affairs, would do, or the doing of something which a reasonable and prudent [person] would not do.* In other words, negligence is the failure to act like a reasonable and prudent person would under the same or similar circumstances. This failure can be manifested in two ways: either by doing something a reasonable and prudent person would not do (an act of commission) or by failing to do something a reasonable and prudent person would have done (an act of omission).

The primary purpose of negligence law is to protect others from unreasonable risks of harm which are foreseeable and therefore preventable. Consequently, under negligence law, the failure to conform one's conduct to that of a reasonable and prudent person is actionable (i.e., results in legal liability) *only if* that failure results in injury to the person or property of another. For example, consider the inattentive driver who runs a stop sign. It is certainly true that a reasonable and prudent person does not run stop signs (in the absence of some extenuating circumstances). However, if there are no other cars or pedestrians on the road, no one is harmed. There is no negligence in this situation because no one was injured. In contrast, if running the stop sign resulted in a collision with another car, there would be property damage to that car and, perhaps, personal injuries to its occupants. In this case, the inattentive driving gives rise to a negligence claim because the failure to act as a reasonable and prudent person caused harm to another.

For a plaintiff to prevail in a negligence lawsuit, he or she must prove (by a preponderance of the evidence) each of the four elements of negligence: 1) the existence of a duty of care, 2) the breach of that duty, 3) proximate cause, and 4) damages.

The duty of care is the obligation to act as the reasonable and prudent person previously discussed. That duty exists if there is a foreseeable risk of harm to others which can be prevented through the exercise of reasonable precautions. If the harm complained of cannot reasonably be foreseen or anticipated, there is no duty. The law does *not* require defendants to be perfect, or to see through crystal balls, it only requires them to act reasonably in light of the probable risk which will result from their activities.

The second element is simply the breach of the duty of care. That is, it is the failure to act as a reasonable and prudent person would under the same or similar circumstances. How does the law define what it means to be a reasonable and prudent person? It does not. Nevertheless, a common sense approach would suggest something like the following: a reasonable and prudent person is someone who simultaneously personifies these characteristics: competent in the field in question, level headed, practical, and fair minded. While none of us personifies all of these qualities at all times, the law's fictionalized person—the reasonable and prudent person—does.

Proximate cause is the third element of negligence. This is the requirement that there be a cause-and-effect relationship between the breach of the duty (the second element) and the damages complained of (the fourth element). Recognizing that this explanation is an oversimplification of the element, proximate cause challenges the plaintiff to prove that the damages complained of would not have occurred were it not for the breach. That is, there were no other circumstances or conditions which would have brought about the damages in question. For example, consider driver A who runs a stop sign and broadsides another car driven by B. B, who is not wearing a seat belt, is thrown from the car and injured. Assume it can be proven that B's injuries would have been much less severe had B been wearing a seat belt. Were B's injuries proximately caused by A's failure to stop for the stop sign (which a reasonable and prudent person would) or by B's failure to wear a seat belt (which a reasonable and prudent person would) or both? This is the type of problem which must be resolved in proving the existence of this element. The answer to the example is the simple two-word statement which, much to the consternation of non-lawyers, correctly answers most legal questions—it depends. What does it depend on? Because this is an issue of negligence law, it depends on the law of each State. Negligence law is a matter of State law (as opposed to Federal law) which means that each State decides for itself how to resolve this type of legal dilemma.

The fourth element of negligence is damages. Damages may take the form of personal injuries (including emotional distress), damage to property, or other general losses such as lost wages. Again, if there are no damages, there is no negligence even if the defendant's conduct was outrageous and, in most instances, would have caused harm.

In product liability lawsuits, negligence may be used as a theory of recovery in either design defect or manufacturing defect cases.

Strict Liability as a Product Liability Theory

Strict liability is a theory of law which imposes liability without regard to any fault, in the usual legal sense, on the part of the defendant. Strict liability is sometimes referred to as absolute liability or liability without fault. It emerged as a theory of law in the early 1960's in response both to the consumer protection movement and to the apparent inability of negligence law to protect injured persons from certain types of inherently dangerous products.

The most frequently cited statement of this rule of law is found in Section 402A of the Restatement (Second) of Torts (1965) which reads as follows:

> 1. One who sells any product in a defective condition *unreasonably dangerous* to the user or consumer or to his property is subject to liability for physical harm thereby caused to the ultimate user or consumer, or to his property if a) the seller is engaged in the business of selling such a product, and b) it is expected to and does reach the user or consumer without substantial change in the condition in which it is sold. (Emphasis added)

2. The rule stated in Subsection (1) applies though a) the seller has exercised all possible care in the preparation and sale of his product, and b) the user or consumer has not bought the product from or entered into any contractual relation with the seller.

The focus of the strict liability theory in a product liability lawsuit is on the product itself. Unlike negligence, where the theory puts the conduct of the defendant(s) under the microscope, strict liability subjects the *product* to intense scrutiny. Under a strict liability theory, a defendant is liable for injuries or damages caused by an *unreasonably dangerous product* even though the defendant *exercised all possible care in its preparation and sale.*

Strict liability is a harsh rule of law. Nevertheless, its evolution can be appreciated by considering the problem it was created to address. While, as noted earlier, it did not emerge as a rule of law until the early 1960's, it was presaged by Justice Traynor in a concurring opinion in a 1944 product liability decision.

In my opinion it should now be recognized that a manufacturer incurs an absolute liability when an article that he has placed on the market, knowing that it is to be used without inspection, proves to have a defect that causes injury to human beings.... Even if there is no negligence, ...public policy demands that responsibility be fixed wherever it will most effectively reduce the hazards of life and health inherent in defective products that reach the market. It is evident that the manufacturer can anticipate some hazards and guard against the recurrence of others, as the public cannot. Those who suffer injury from defective products are unprepared to meet its consequences. The cost of an injury and the loss of time or health may be an overwhelming misfortune to the person injured, and a needless one, for the risk of injury can be insured by the manufacturer and distributed among the public as a cost of doing business. It is to the public interest to discourage the marketing of products having defects that are a menace to the public. If such products nevertheless find their way into the market it is to the public interest to place the responsibility for whatever injury they may cause upon the manufacturer, who, even if he is not negligent in the manufacture of the product, is responsible for its reaching the market. However intermittently such injuries may occur and however haphazardly they may strike, the risk of their occurrence is a constant risk and a general one. Against such a risk there should be a general and constant protection and the manufacturer is best situated to afford such protection.... While the Legislature imposes criminal liability [without fault] only with regard to food products and their containers, there are many other sources of danger. It is to the public interest to prevent injury to the public from any defective goods by the imposition of civil liability generally.... As handicrafts have been replaced by mass production with its great markets and transportation facilities, the close relationship between the producer and consumer of a product has been altered. Manufacturing processes, frequently valuable secrets, are ordinarily either inaccessible to or beyond the ken of the general public. The consumer no longer has means or skill enough to investigate for himself the soundness of a product, even when it is not contained in a sealed package, and his erstwhile vigilance has been lulled by the steady efforts of manufacturers to build up confidence by advertising and marketing devices such as trademarks.... Consumers no longer approach products warily but accept them on faith, relying on the reputation of the manufacturer or the trademark.... Manufacturers have sought to justify that faith by increasingly high standards of inspection and a readiness to make good on defective products by way of replacements and refunds.... The manufacturer's obligation to the consumer must keep pace with the changing relationship between them; it cannot be escaped because the marketing of a product has become so complicated as to require one or more intermediaries. The manufacturer's liability should, of course, be defined in terms of the safety of the product in normal and proper use, and should not extend to injuries that cannot be traced to the product as it reached the market. *Escola v. Coca Cola Bottling Co.*, 24 Cal.2d 453, 150 P.2d 436 (1944) (concurring opinion).

Justice Traynor recognized the inequity that existed between manufacturers and sellers, on the one hand, and buyers and other users of consumer products, on the other. Gone were the days of relative equality in bargaining power and knowledge of the item purchased. Given the manufacturer's and seller's superior position, sound public policy compelled a tougher standard of accountability for placing dangerous products in the hands of the public. However, both the Restatement of Torts and Justice Traynor left room for the defendants to absolve themselves of liability by showing: 1) the product was substantially changed after it was sold, or 2) it was used in some abnormal or improper way.

The Implied Warranty of Merchantability as a Product Liability Theory

The implied warranty of merchantability is a contract-based theory found in Article 2 (Sales) of the Uniform Commercial Code. It is similar to strict liability in that it predicates liability on the basis that a product is not reasonably safe. Implied warranties stand in contrast to express warranties. Express warranties are labelled "express" because they are specifically stated—usually in writing—but express warranties can be stated orally. Implied warranties are not stated but are implied by operation of law. In other words, implied warranties exist because the law says so. Sellers subject to the implied warranty provisions do not have to do or say anything to extend these guarantees; they are extended to consumers and other users of products by statute. (In some cases, implied warranties can be limited or excluded. This will be discussed later.)

The implied warranty of merchantability is found at Article 2-

214 of the Uniform Commercial Code. In relevant part, it reads as follows:

1. Unless excluded or modified, a warranty that the goods shall be merchantable is implied in a contract for their sale if a seller is a merchant with respect to goods of that kind....

2. Goods to be merchantable must be at least...fit for the ordinary purposes for which...[such goods] are used....

The basic requirement of the implied warranty of merchantability is that the product is *fit for the ordinary purposes* for which that product is normally used. For example, a power saw must be able to cut wood because that is what it is supposed to do. If it will not cut a wedding cake, there is no liability under this theory because that is not one of its ordinary purposes.

Examples of Design Defect Cases

Hagans v. Oliver Machinery Company and *Fahey v. Rockwell Graphic Systems, Inc., & Another* are two sample cases which examined claims of design defects. *Hagans* involved claims under negligence and strict liability theories. *Fahey* alleged liability under negligence and the implied warranty of merchantability. Like the other cases which will be used, *Hagans* and *Fahey* are appeals court decisions. That is, the trial court entered a judgment and the losing party appealed that judgment to the next higher court. As a point of clarification, it is important to be aware that appeals courts can consider issues of law only. That is, the trial court is the finder of fact (i.e., it decides what happened). With very limited exceptions, the only thing an appeals court can do is determine whether or not the law was applied correctly. It cannot, for example, examine the conflicting testimony of the two parties and second guess the trial court as to which party was telling the truth.

In *Hagans*, the trial court ruled in favor of the plaintiff. The defendant appealed that ruling to the appeals court. The essence of the appeal was that the trial court erred because the evidence was inconsistent with the result.

While reading these cases, there is a number of things to pay attention to. Which facts do the appeals court find relevant to its conclusion? What similarities exist between the court's analysis of a strict liability claim versus a negligence claim versus an implied warranty of merchantability claim? In *Hagans*, how does it deal with a product which was manufactured in 1942, but produced an injury in 1971? How does the court balance the interests of both sides to the dispute? What weight does the court give to existing standards for such products? What does the court have to say about "deep pockets" and sympathetic plaintiffs?

The following cases, along with other cases presented later, appear in edited form. That is, portions of the actual case have been omitted for the sake of clarity. Similarly, in most instances, legal citations appearing in the body of the opinion have been omitted. In addition, headings have been appropriately inserted for ease of reading. Some of these cases will be referred to later in relation to other issues of law.

HAGANS v. OLIVER MACHINERY COMPANY
U.S. Court of Appeals (5th Circuit)
576 F.2d 97 (1978)

Facts: In this products liability action, the plaintiff (Hagans) recovered a $50,000 jury verdict for injuries sustained while operating an industrial table saw manufactured 30 years before by the defendant Oliver Machinery Company.

Defendant Oliver Machinery Company is a leading manufacturer of industrial woodcutting equipment, including commercial table saws. The saw involved in this case, a 2000 pound tilting arbor miter saw designed for industrial use, was manufactured by defendant in 1942 and delivered to the United States Navy. Shortly after World War II, the saw was sold to Century Machinery Company, who in 1960 resold the machine to plaintiff's employer, Utility Trailer Company of El Paso, Texas.

On October 11, 1971, plaintiff seriously injured his left hand while operating the saw. According to plaintiff, he was feeding a board into the saw when the circular blade hit a knot in the wood, causing the board to jerk up abruptly. As the board descended, plaintiff's left hand, which he had been using to steady the board, fell onto the circular blade. Plaintiff's ring finger was completely severed and his middle finger severely lacerated as a result of the accident.

Plaintiff sued in federal district court on theories of strict liability and negligent design, contending that the saw should have been equipped with permanent safety devices or with adequate warnings of the dangerous nature of the machine. After a two-day trial, a jury returned a $50,000 verdict for plaintiff. Defendant appeals, arguing that the district court erred in denying defendant's motions for a directed verdict and for judgment notwithstanding the verdict.

When sold by defendant in 1942, the saw was equipped with a guard assembly that fit over the saw blade. Incorporated into the guard assembly was an antikickback device that prevented the wood from being thrown back by the saw blade at the operator. Because certain important operations could not be performed on the saw with the guard in place, it was designed to be removable. The saw was apparently still equipped with this safety device when sold to plaintiff's employer in 1960, but the guard was not attached to the saw when plaintiff was injured. The record contains no indication when or why the safety device was removed. It is undisputed that plaintiff's injury would have been avoided had the blade guard been attached.

Design Defect Under Strict Liability Theory: Under the theory of products liability expressed in Section 402A of the Restatement (Second) of Torts and adopted by the Supreme Court of Texas, a manufacturer who sells a product in a "defective condition unreasonably dangerous" is strictly liable for physical harm caused by the defect to the product's user even though the manufacturer "has exercised all possible care in the preparation and sale of his product." A product is "unreasonably dangerous" only if it is "defective," whether designed defectively or improperly and produced as designed, or designed perfectly but improperly or defectively produced.

Because many products have both utility and danger, the alleged defect is required to render the offending product "unreasonably dangerous" before strict liability is imposed. A product is unreasonably dangerous if its utility does not outweigh the magnitude of the danger inherent in its introduction into commerce.

In balancing utility against danger, the court must not monocularly view the scales from the standpoint of either the user, whose injury convinces him positively that the product is unreasonably dangerous, or the manufacturer, whose profit motive may unduly interfere with his objective evaluation of the product's dangers. Rather, the court is required to consider the legitimate interests of both sides, cognizant that the user is entitled to expect that the product has been properly designed to meet the demands of its intended and proper usage without deficiencies rendering it unreasonably dangerous, but also cognizant that the manufacturer is not an insurer of his product, charged by the law to design every part to be the best science can produce or to guarantee that no harm will come to the user. The standard to be applied in the balancing process can thus be expressed from the perspectives of both seller and user: a product is defective and unreasonably dangerous if a reasonable seller aware of the dangers involved would not sell the product or if the risk of injury exceeds that contemplated by an ordinary and reasonable consumer.

In evaluating a manufacturer's liability for injuries caused by his inevitably hazardous product, a court must first determine whether the product is so unsafe that marketing it at all is "unreasonably dangerous per se" and, if not, then determine whether the product has been introduced into the stream of commerce without sufficient safeguards, thus rendering it "unreasonably dangerous as marketed."

Plaintiff Hagans argued to the jury that the removable blade guard assembly should have been designed into the saw as an unremovable safety feature through welding, rivets, or other means of permanent attachment. In support of this contention, plaintiff produced evidence that defendant had known in 1942 that commercial table saws annually accounted for a large number of industrial accidents, that technology was available in 1942 to permanently attach the blade guard assembly to the saw, and the plaintiff's injury would have been avoided had the saw been equipped with the blade guard.

Defendant introduced evidence that in 1942 the saw exceeded industry safety practices and national and associational safety standards, that few competing manufacturers of commercial table saws included blade guards of any kind as standard equipment, and that as of the time of the injury no competitor manufactured an industrial table saw equipped with a permanently affixed blade guard. More importantly, it was undisputed that permanent attachment of the blade guard assembly would substantially limit the saw's usefulness. Common woodworking functions such as dadoing and rabbeting could not be performed on the saw with the guard in position. Indeed, the safety device had to be removed in order to straight-cut pieces of lumber of certain widths. As defense expert witness Professor Ralph Barnett observed, if the blade guard assembly had been welded or otherwise permanently attached to the saw, "[y]ou would wind up with a commercial...heavy-duty industrial machine which is not capable of cutting the most ordinary four by eight sheet of plywood...." Plaintiff offered no evidence that in 1942 a permanent guard assembly could have been devised which would protect the operator during every woodworking operation performable on the saw.

A finding for plaintiff on the issue of defective design ignores the fact that "[s]afety is not the only criterion a manufacturer considers when designing a product." When designing the saw at issue here, the Oliver Machinery Company was faced with the difficult task of reconciling its safety concerns with the realities of a competitive marketplace. It has three basic alternatives. At one extreme, defendant could, as many of its competitors apparently did, market a commercial table saw without any blade guard assembly as standard equipment. At the other extreme, the company could have done as plaintiff suggests: permanently weld or rivet the blade guard assembly in place on the saw. In so doing, however, defendant would render his product incapable of performing many important woodworking functions that could be performed by saws marketed by his competitors.

Finally, recognizing that potential customers for its product expect industrial table saws to perform a wide range of woodworking operations, and that some of those operations cannot be performed with a blade guard assembly in position on the saw, defendant elected the third basic alternative available to it: equipping the saw with a removable blade guard assembly. So equipped, the saw is capable of performing the wide range of woodworking operations expected of it, while at the same time providing the blade guard's protection for those operations which can be performed with a blade guard in place. By designing the saw with a removable blade guard, defendant struck a compromise that maximized the product's utility and safety.

Industrial woodcutting tools are essential to many American industries. In particular, the construction industry is a cornerstone of the American economy and a major contributor to the standard of living in this country. Unfortunately, the nature of the industry is such that its tools, from the smallest tack hammer to the largest earth mover, expose certain risks of harm to their users. Nevertheless, unless civilization is to grind to a halt, these tools, including industrial table saws, must continue to be marketed despite their inherent dangers. Clearly, therefore, defendant's product is not unreasonably dangerous per se.

Nor is the industrial table saw manufactured by defendant unreasonably dangerous as marketed. The evidence is overwhelming that permanent attachment of the blade guard assembly would seriously impair the usefulness of defendant's product. Texas law does not require a manufacturer to destroy the utility of his product in order to make it safe. On the issue of defective design, the district court should have directed a verdict for defendant.

Design Defect Under Negligence Theory: Like his strict liability claims, plaintiff's negligence claims were based on defendant's failure to attach the blade guard to the saw in a permanent manner and defendant's failure to warn users of the dangers associated with using the saw without a blade guard.

It is well settled that a manufacturer is under a duty to use reasonable care in designing his product so that it is reasonably safe for its intended use. The crucial inquiry in negligent design cases is the question of reasonableness. "The defendant is not obliged to design the safest possible product, or one as safe as others make or a safer product than the one he has designed, so long as the design he has adopted is reasonably safe."

At trial, plaintiff introduced evidence that defendant had been aware in 1942 of the high number of injuries caused by industrial table saws, that defendant could have foreseen that its saws would be used without the blade guards in position, and that the blade guard would have prevented plaintiff's injury. This evidence, according to plaintiff, was sufficient to prove that defendant was negligent in not permanently affixing the blade guard in position on the saw.

Defendant, in contrast, produced evidence that it has been a leader in the woodworking industry since 1937 and that its products have always exceeded industry safety practices and associational and national safety standards. Indeed, defendant's saw, built in 1942, was shown to comport with current OSHA safety standards for comparable machines. Additionally, defendant produced evidence that its product was among the safest saws on the market in 1942, and that at the time of trial no manufacturer had produced a table saw with a permanently attached blade guard. Finally, it was undisputed that adoption of plaintiff's suggested design alternative would virtually destroy the saw's usefulness as an industrial woodworking tool.

Acceptance of plaintiff's theory in this case would go far toward imposing absolute liability on manufacturers for all product-related injuries. A manufacturer need not incorporate into his product safety features that render the product incapable of performing some or all of the very functions creating its public demand. Plaintiff was entitled to a reasonably safe product, not an unreasonably safe product.

As we concluded in the discussion on strict liability, equipping the saw with a removable blade guard assembly was a manifestly reasonable melding of utility and safety. On the evidence contained in this record, reasonable men could not conclude that Oliver Machinery Company was negligent in designing an unreasonably dangerous saw.

Conclusion: As a result of his unfortunate accident, Curtis Hagans has suffered a serious, permanent physical injury, an injury that arouses in us, no less than in the jury, a deep sense of sympathy. Our recognition, however, that one of the parties has the powerful influence of sympathy on his side prompts us to scrutinize the record all the more closely, for only the most naive could deny that compassion, one of the strongest and most admirable human emotions, can sometimes cloud a jury's perception of the evidence and facts presented, and could lead it to hold liable for legally cognizable wrongs one who has committed none. The tendency of sympathetic jurors, although well intentioned, to confuse liability with ability to bear loss forms the basis of the rule of law allowing the judge to deprive the jury of its right to decide against the defendant. That the jury has wrongfully held an innocent defendant liable is not lightly to be assumed, however; only "[i]f the facts and inferences point so strongly and overwhelming in favor of [defendant] that the Court believes that reasonable men could not arrive at a contrary verdict" may a motion for directed verdict or judgment notwithstanding the verdict be granted in favor of defendant. The record before us leads inescapably to the conclusion that this was such a case.

In *Fahey,* the trial court entered a directed verdict for the defendants, and the plaintiff is appealing. That is, the trial court concluded that there was not enough evidence to go to the trouble of even giving it to the jury; so the judge summarily ruled in favor of the defendants. The plaintiff claims this was an error, that there was enough evidence to support the plaintiff's side of the case, and that the jury should have been allowed to deliberate.

Fahey involves claims of negligence and the violation of the implied warranty of merchantability. In a design defect context, an implied warranty of merchantability claim is based on the theory that a defectively designed product cannot be fit for the ordinary purposes for which such products are used.

FAHEY v. ROCKWELL GRAPHIC SYSTEMS, INC., & ANOTHER
Massachusetts Appeals Court
20 Mass. App. Ct. 642 (1985)

Facts: On January 24, 1977, Robert W. Fahey, a pressman employed by Acme Printing Company (Acme), sustained injuries to his right arm when it was pulled into and crushed by a printing press designed and manufactured by the defendant Roland Offsetmaschinenfabrik (Roland) and distributed by the defendant Rockwell Graphic Systems, Inc. (Rockwell). Fahey and his wife sought damages against Roland and Rockwell on theories of negligent design and breach of warranty.... At the close of the plaintiff's case before a Superior Court jury, the judge directed verdicts for the defendants. The plaintiff's appeal from the ensuing judgments, arguing error in the allowance of the motions for directed verdicts....

We summarize the evidence.... As originally designed and manufactured, the printing press was equipped with a guard to protect press operators from a nip point, an in-running juncture between two adjacent cylinders moving in opposite directions. The guard was designed to shield the nip point and automatically stop the press when touched. It was screwed into place and was not designed to be removed for press operations or maintenance. On the day of Fahey's injury, however, the guard was not on the press. It had been removed by Fahey some three weeks earlier.

The guard was affixed to the main frame of the press, an apparently unusual location. On other presses, it was attached to the lower unit inker. Although the guard adequately shielded the nip point, its location had the effect of decreasing productivity by interfering with the efficient mounting of press plates. It forced the pressman to stand off-balance while changing plates, and necessitated the efforts of two pressmen for plate mounting when previously one had sufficed. The guard's location also resulted in plate scratching and interference with press greasing. Due to the guard's position, it took half an hour to change plates (make-ready time). By comparison, on a press on which the guard was attached to the lower unit inker, that operation took only five minutes. This delay added approximately one hour to each make-ready time, which over the course of a week could amount to five or more additional hours in production time. The result was that Fahey was unable to meet management's expected make-ready time.

Fahey and his assistant pressman, Michael McCorry, alerted Acme to these problems. Fahey similarly complained to Aime Carrier, a Rockwell employee whose duties included installing and servicing presses distributed by Rockwell and instructing pressmen on the operations and functions of the presses. Fahey told Carrier that he wanted to move the guard because its location increased make-ready time and caused scratching on the plates. Later, Carrier notified Rockwell concerning this complaint.

Soon after Fahey's conversation with Carrier, Fahey and McCorry took the guard off the press by removing a number of screws. This procedure, by Fahey's own estimate, took approximately fifteen to twenty minutes. With the guard removed, the nip point between the two cylinders was fully exposed.

Approximately three weeks after removing the guard, Fahey attempted to remove a hickey from a plate with his thumb while the press was in operation. Removing hickies on plates by this method was a common technique for pressmen. Fahey had used the method "hundreds" of times without incident. While he was attempting to remove the hickey, the nip point caught Fahey's hand, pulling his arm between the cylinders and crushing it. Had the guard been in place at the time of the accident, the nip point would have been inaccessible, and the guard, if touched, would have tripped a switch, shutting down the press.

At the time of his injury, Fahey had been working at Acme for ten years. For three of those years he had been an assistant pressman. Later, he was promoted to the position of pressman and exercised supervisory responsibilities over a press crew. He had been a pressman for four years at the time of his injury. He had, however, worked on this particular type of press for only one month prior to the time he removed the guard.

Fahey knew the danger of an exposed, in-running nip point. He admitted that had the guard been in place, his hand could not have reached the nip point. He recognized that the nip point presented "some danger" but was unaware of the potential for "grave danger" and serious injury. Fahey did not know that his arm would be pulled into the machine and was unaware of the magnitude of harm that would ensue.

Fahey never read any safety bulletin concerning press operations. He could not recall ever having been instructed by his employer regarding safety precautions. He was "generally aware" of posted warnings on the press which, among other things, cautioned:

> "BE SURE PRESS IS COMPLETELY STOPPED
> BEFORE TOUCHING
> ANY OPERATING PART OF THE PRESS."

> "ALL GUARDS AND COVERS
> MUST BE SECURELY LOCKED IN PLACE
> WHEN PRESS IS IN OPERATION."

The guard could have been located on the lower unit inker instead of the main press frame. In fact, following Fahey's injury, Rockwell had the guard moved from the main frame to the lower unit inker on both this press and other presses. Attached to the lower unit inker, the guard covered the nip point equally well, increased efficiency, and posed no disadvantage. The guard could also have been equipped with interlocks.

An essential safety design principle of nip point guarding is to make the hazard inaccessible. This involves a recognition that if a guard interferes with a press operator's tasks, it is likely to be removed. Whenever possible, a guard should be designed so that it cannot be removed, or placed so that there will no incentive to remove it.

Negligent Design Theory: A manufacturer is under a duty to design a machine with reasonable care, and is held to the standard of an ordinary reasonably prudent designer in like circumstances. The product must be designed with reasonable care to eliminate avoidable dangers. It is, therefore, incumbent on the designer to "anticipate the environment in which its product will be used, and...design against the reasonably foreseeable risks attending the product's use in that setting." This expansive duty reflects a social policy of casting an "increased responsibility upon the manufacturer, who stands in a superior position to recognize and cure defects, for improper conduct in the placement of finished products into channels of commerce.

Designing a product that functions as intended, is accompanied by warnings, and whose danger is obvious will not necessarily preclude a finding of liability for negligent design. "[T]here is a case for the jury if the plaintiff can show an available design modification which would reduce the risk without undue cost or interference with the performance of the machinery." In evaluating the adequacy of a product's design, the jury must weigh "the gravity of the danger posed by the challenged design, the likelihood that such danger would occur, the mechanical feasibility of a safer alternative design, the financial cost of an improved design, and the adverse consequences to the product and to the consumer that would result from an alternative design."

The evidence in this case warranted findings that: 1) the placement of the guard significantly increased production time, caused the pressman to stand off-balance while changing plates, resulted in plate scratching and interfered with press greasing; 2) an essential principle of press safety design is a recognition that guards that interfere with pressmen's tasks are likely to be removed; 3) removal of the guard on this press would expose a dangerous nip point; and 4) pressmen commonly remove hickies by hand on operating presses. Thus, there was sufficient evidence to take the case to the jury on the question whether the circumstances of the guard's removal and the plaintiff's subsequent injury were reasonably foreseeable.

There was also sufficient evidence for the jury to determine "the gravity of the danger posed by the challenged design, the likelihood such danger would occur, the mechanical feasibility of a safer alternative design, the financial cost of an improved design, and the adverse consequences to the product and to the consumer that would result from an alternative design." First, because the potential injury from the exposed nip point might be serious, it was not necessary that the likelihood of accident be high to warrant the careful design of safety features on the press. As to an alternative location for the guard, there was evidence of the feasibility of attaching the guard to the lower unit inker, and evidence that the guard was attached to the lower unit inker on other presses, including the press in question following Fahey's injury. There was evidence that had the guard been attached to the lower unit inker, it would have shielded the nip point equally well, increased productivity, and posed no disadvantage. There was also evidence that the cost of locating the guard on the lower unit inker would have been minimal. As to the issue of interlocks, there was evidence that the guard could have been interlocked, but that a nondefeatable interlocking system would have been complex and would have added "appreciable expense." There was sufficient evidence for the jury to make a "judgment as to the social acceptability of the design."

Rockwell argues that it cannot be held liable for negligent design because it did not design the press. That argument ignores the rule of Restatement (Second) of Torts Section 400 (1965) that "[o]ne who puts out as his own product a chattel manufactured by another is subject to the same liability as though he were its manufacturer." Comment d to Section 400 explains that, when an actor appears to be the manufacturer of a product, he "frequently causes the chattel to be used in reliance upon his care in making it.... Thus, one puts out a chattel as his own product when he puts it out under his name."

The evidence introduced by the plaintiffs showed the following. Roland manufactured and designed the press. It was labeled a "Miehle-Roland" press. Literature described the press as a "Miehle-Roland" press and extolled in detail the technological advances in press design which it offered. Miehle was a division of and "the same as" Rockwell.

We think the evidence was sufficient to provide a basis for the jury to find that Rockwell put the press out as its own product (at least as a comanufacturer with Roland) and, therefore, to subject Rockwell to liability for negligent design. It was error to direct a verdict for Rockwell on Fahey's negligent design theory.

The Breach of Warranty Theory: Under G.L.c. 106, Sections 2-314 to 2-318, both Roland and Rockwell impliedly warranted that the press was "fit for the ordinary purposes for which such [presses] are used...[including] both those uses which [they] intended and those which are reasonably foreseeable." It is now settled that the law of implied warranty in Massachusetts is "congruent in nearly all respects with the principles [strict liability] expressed in Restatement (Second) of Torts Section 402A (1965)." In deciding the issue of warranty liability, "the jury must weigh competing factors much as they would in determining the fault of the defendant in a negligence case. The inquiry focuses on product characteristics rather than on the defendant's conduct, but the nature of the decision is essentially the same. In evaluating the adequacy of a product's design, the jury should consider, among other factors, 'the gravity of the danger posed by the challenged design, the likelihood that such danger would occur, the mechanical feasibility of a safer alternative design, the financial cost of an improved design, and the adverse consequences to the product and to the consumer that would result from an alternative design.'"

We have determined in part 1 of this opinion that there was sufficient evidence to take the case to the jury on design negligence. Under the holding of *Hayes v. Ariens* (that a defendant cannot be found to have been negligent without having been in breach of the warranty of merchantability), it follows that there was sufficient evidence to withstand the defendant's motions for directed verdicts on the warranty counts.

Conclusion: The judgments...are reversed....

Manufacturing Defect Cases

Theories of Liability
While design defect cases focus on the manner in which a

product was supposed to be manufactured, manufacturing defect cases focus on the actual product as it was delivered by the manufacturer. Generally, manufacturing defect cases claim some combination of the following: a defect existed in the production process, design specifications were not followed, or improper or inadequate instructions or warnings rendered the product defective. These claims may be made concerning only one unit of the product (e.g., the car which turns out to be a lemon) or about an entire production run of the same product.

The theories of law used in manufacturing defect cases are the same as those used in design defect cases: negligence, strict liability, and the implied warranty of merchantability. Regardless of the theory of law used, a plaintiff must establish that the manufacturer produced an unreasonably unsafe product in light of the reasonably foreseeable uses and dangers inherent in its nature.

Examples of Manufacturing Defect Cases

H.P. Hood & Sons, Inc. v Ford Motor Co. is an example of a manufacturing defect case in which negligence is used as the theory of liability. In this case, Hood and one of its employees are suing Ford and the dealership for injuries suffered by the employee when the steering failed in a new Ford truck. The portion of the case excerpted here deals only with the liability of Ford and the dealership to the employee. In concluding that there was sufficient evidence to find that the defendants were negligent in relation to the employee's injuries, the court examines the relationship between negligence law (a common law doctrine) and Federal statutory law regarding manufacturers' obligations to notify customers of unsafe products and to institute recall programs.

H.P. HOOD & SONS, INC. v. FORD MOTOR COMPANY

Massachusetts S.J.C.

370 Mass. 69 (1976)

Facts: This is an action in tort...brought originally by H.P. Hood &

Sons, Inc. (Hood), and its employee, William Terranova, against Ford Motor Company (Ford), and Toby Ford Sales, Inc. (Toby), to recover for injuries to person and property sustained by the plaintiffs when Terranova was involved in a motor vehicle collision in the course of his employment with Hood. At the time of the collision, he was operating a truck which had been manufactured by Ford and sold by its dealer Toby to Hood.

We summarize the evidence most favorable to Terranova on this issue. Terranova was employed by Hood as a truck driver. The truck which was assigned to him and which he regularly drove was one of a number of such vehicles manufactured by Ford and purchased by Hood from Toby, a Ford dealer. On June 7, 1968, Terranova was operating the truck in the course of his employment. As he drove the truck up a hill at a speed of about twenty-five to thirty miles an hour, "all of a sudden something violent happened in the truck. The steering wheel was torn from [his] hands, and then [he] had a tremendous sensation of going to the right, just violently going to the right...." Terranova was buffeted about the cab of the truck, temporarily losing consciousness, and the truck turned over onto its side and came to a stop.

An expert witness called by the plaintiffs testified that in his opinion the accident was caused by a right front spring hanger bracket on the truck which was improperly fastened and which separated from the frame rail. The witness testified further that this condition "allowed the right front wheel to be displaced rearward, where it contacted the inside of the right front wheel well...[that t]his motion of the right front wheel rearward forced the vehicle into a sharp right turn, [that t]he vehicle subsequently rode over its own wheel and axle assembly at the rear of the right front wheel, [and that t]his forced the right front of the vehicle up into the air and caused this truck to roll over with its left side down." He testified in addition that the defective condition of the rivets which caused the improper fastening of the front spring hanger bracket was "strictly a manufacturing defect."

An expert witness called by Ford testified that such defective rivets should have been discoverable by an inspector at Ford and that the inspection process at Ford failed to the extent that Ford vehicles were distributed with malformed rivets. It further appeared from the evidence that as of the date of the accident the truck had been driven no more than 1,637 miles and that prior to the accident Terranova had never experienced any mechanical difficulty with the truck nor noticed anything unusual about it.

The evidence summarized above was sufficient to warrant a finding that Ford had been negligent in manufacturing the defective truck and in failing to discover such defect by reasonable inspection. The jury so found. Indeed, Ford appears not to dispute this finding, arguing instead that it should be held as [a] matter of law to have proved a valid defense to the action on a showing of good faith compliance with relevant provisions of the National Traffic and Motor Vehicle Safety Act of 1966...and a demonstration that it has made reasonable provisions for free repairs of defects covered by a vehicle recall program instituted by it. We disagree.

Negligence Claim: At all times relevant to this case, [applicable Federal law], provided in pertinent part as follows: "(a)...Every manufacturer of motor vehicles shall furnish notification of any defect in any motor vehicle or motor vehicle equipment produced by manufacturer which he [the manufacturer] determines, in good faith, relates to motor vehicle safety, to the purchaser (where known to the manufacturer) of such motor vehicle or motor vehicle equipment, within a reasonable time after such manufacturer has discovered such defect.... "(c)...The notification required by subsection (a) of this section shall contain a clear description of such defect, an evaluation of the risk to traffic safety reasonably related to such defect, and a statement of the measures to be taken to repair such defect." It is clear that Ford did furnish Hood with the notification of the possibility that the Ford trucks purchased by Hood contained a defect relating to motor vehicle safety. Such notification was accomplished by means of a letter,...and a series of conferences between representatives of Ford and Hood. Terranova raises a question, which we need not decide, as to the sufficiency under the statute of notification provided by Ford. Even assuming that Ford's notification was in full compliance with the Federal standards, such compliance in and of itself does not establish a defense to this action at common law. As provided in [the applicable Federal statute]: "Compliance with any Federal motor vehicle safety standard issued under this subchapter does not exempt any person from liability under common law."…. "It is apparent that the National Traffic [and Motor Vehicle] Safety Act [of 1966] is intended to be supplementary of and in addition to the common law of negligence and product liability."

Under the law of this Commonwealth, a manufacturer of a product, which the manufacturer knows or should know is dangerous by nature or is in a dangerous condition, owes a duty to exercise reasonable care to prevent injury to those persons who it is foreseeable will come in contact with, and consequently be endangered by, that product…. Moreover, "[t]he duty to exercise reasonable care includes a duty to warn of danger, if 'the person on whom that duty rests has some reason to suppose a warning is needed.'" …On the evidence presented at trial, it was properly left to the jury to decide whether the steps taken by Ford to warn of the risks of danger posed by the defective truck were sufficient to satisfy the duty which Ford owed at common law.

Moreover, a jury issue was also presented as to whether a so-called "Service Campaign H-35," a program instituted by Ford to recall and repair trucks suspected of containing defective rivets, and Ford's offer to provide repairs for Hood trucks pursuant thereto, fulfilled Ford's common law duty to exercise reasonable care to prevent injury to persons to whom a risk of harm was foreseeable…. There was evidence that representatives of Ford and Hood entered into negotiations relative to repair of the trucks, that Ford offered to provide repair kits, containing the parts necessary to repair the trucks, to Hood through its dealer Toby and to reimburse Hood for labor which Hood mechanics performed in remedying the defective condition of the trucks, and that Hood did not undertake to make such repairs. There was also evidence that the repair kits made available to Hood were incomplete and did not contain parts sufficient to carry out the necessary repairs. On this evidence, the question whether Ford exercised reasonable care was again properly one for the jury to decide. The evidence was sufficient to warrant the jury in finding, as they did, that Ford was negligent. That Hood itself may have been negligent (as may be implied from the jury's finding against Hood in its count for negligence against Ford) in no way relieves Ford of liability to Terranova for its negligence in the circumstances of this case.... Judgment [is] to be entered in accordance with the verdict of the jury.

The implied warranty of merchantability is a second theory employed in manufacturing defect cases. *Taterka v. Ford Motor Company* is an example of its application. (It is purely coincidental that two cases against Ford were used here.) In this case, Ford prevailed in persuading the court that it did not violate the warranty.

TATERKA v. FORD MOTOR COMPANY
Supreme Court of Wisconsin
271 N.W.2d 653 (1978)

Facts: On September 20, 1971, Taterka entered into a contract to purchase a 1972 Ford Mustang from a Milwaukee Ford dealer. Taterka took delivery of the car on January 14, 1972. At that time, he was given an owner's manual and a Warranty Facts booklet. In October 1974, Taterka discovered that the taillight assembly gaskets had been installed in a way which permitted water to enter causing rust to form. On November 7, 1974, Taterka notified Ford of this rust problem by contacting Ford's Boston district office. Ford did not take any action to correct the problem and Taterka commenced this action on July 28, 1975.

The record reflects Ford had recognized that it had a rust problem with its 1969–1972 model cars. On August 25, 1972, General Field Bulletin No. 550 was issued by Ford authorizing Ford's regional and district managers to provide coverage for rust repairs in response to individual customer complaints. This service program would pay 100 percent of the repair costs up to 24 months and 75 percent from 24 to 36 months. Dealers were not notified of the program.

Taterka also introduced other Ford documents concerning the rust problem. On[e] report dated October 19, 1973, indicated that the "General Product Acceptance Specification" (GPAS) permitted no "metal perforation on exterior appearance panels" for five years. The report observed that Ford's products seemed competitive for the one- and two-year requirements but otherwise did not satisfy the GPAS in a "severe corrosion environment" because perforations developed one to two years earlier in Fords than in competitor's automobiles.

In a decision dated June 15, 1976, granting Ford's motion for summary judgment, the trial court concluded that Taterka's claim was without merit because the auto was merchantable. The court stated:

> ...It seems to the Court that to state the facts is to dispose of the case. A manufacturer is not expected to manufacture an automobile that is perfect in every detail nor is he expected to manufacture an automobile that operates indefinitely. This automobile, having been driven 90,000 miles, has used up approximately most of its useful life. Certainly it cannot be claimed that the automobile was not merchantable at the time of the purchase.

Implied Warranty of Merchantability Claim: Merchantability is defined in [Wisconsin law as follows:] "(2) Goods to be merchantable must be at least such as: (a) Pass without objection in the trade under the contract description; and...(c) Are fit for the ordinary purposes for which such goods are used;..." A finding of merchantability requires an examination of the defects alleged to exist in the particular product in light of the standard of quality expected for that product.

The issue of merchantability presents an issue of fact. The question to be answered is whether conflicting inferences can be drawn from the undisputed facts.

Taterka alleged manufacturing defects including improper corrosion treatment and installation of taillight assembly gaskets. This allegation was supported by a newspaper article on the Ford rust problem, an affidavit from a body shop owner, and Ford's own research reports on the rusting. Ford denied this allegation of manufacturing defects but did not respond with counteraffidavits. Ford also argues that the automobile's merchantability...[was] demonstrated by the fact that it was driven as a personal vehicle in excess of 75,000 miles.

Where automobiles are concerned, the term "unmerchantable" has only been applied where a single defect poses a substantial safety hazard, or numerous defects classify the car as a "lemon."...The ordinary purpose for which a car is intended is to provide transportation. Where a car can provide safe, reliable transportation, it is generally considered merchantable.

The automobile here involved had been driven for 33 months and in excess of 75,000 miles without a serious misadventure. In fact, it had been driven 90,000 miles at the time of the hearing...in 1976. The only inference that can reasonably be drawn from the undisputed facts is that the rust problem described in this case did not render the car unfit for the purpose of driving and therefore unmerchantable.... Judgment affirmed.

Strict liability is the final theory typically utilized in manufacturing defect cases. As noted earlier, the essence of a strict liability case is that the product was defective in a manner which rendered it *unreasonably dangerous* for use by a consumer. *Coca Cola Bottling Company of Houston v. Hobart,* 423 S.W.2d 118 (Appls. Ct. of Texas, 1968), is a case which utilized both negligence and strict liability theories. Only the strict liability theory will be discussed here. Mrs. Hobart cut her finger when attempting to open a coke bottle. The essence of the strict liability claim was that the bottle must have been defective because the level of force she exerted in opening the bottle was not sufficient to cause it to break; and, in addition, there was evidence that the bottle had not been mishandled by Mrs. Hobart. While the court agreed with these findings, it nonetheless ruled for Coca Cola on this issue. In finding for the defendant, the court pointed out that in addition to proving that Mrs. Hobart did not mishandle the product, it was also necessary to prove that no one else in the chain of distribution mishandled the product. That is, for liability to attach to the bottling company, it must be proven that the bottle was defective when it left the bottling plant. The court found in this case that the evidence was inadequate to prove that it was defective at that point of departure. The defect could have been the result of mishandling by the supermarket from which the product was purchased. In addition to illustrating the use of strict liability as a theory in manufacturing defect cases, this case points out the difficulty plaintiffs encounter when suing a manufacturer directly. The burden of proving that the defect existed at the time the product left the plant is a serious obstacle to overcome.

Misrepresentation Cases

Introduction

The underlying problem in misrepresentation cases is that the product fails to conform to that which was represented. At this point, the term misrepresentation is being used in a general lay sense. That is, it refers to a factual discrepancy between the actual nature and/or quality of the product and what the customer was led to believe. This should not be confused with the tort of misrepresentation which is one of the three theories which will be discussed in this section. The other theories which may be used in this type of case are warranty theories found in the Uniform Commercial Code: express warranty and the implied warranty of fitness for a particular purpose.

Express Warranty as a Product Liability Theory

The law governing express warranties is found at Article 2-313 of the Uniform Commercial Code. There is no provision in the U.C.C. which requires a designer, manufacturer, or seller to give a consumer any express warranties. In general, what it does say is that *if* representations are made concerning the characteristics or performance capacity of a product, then the product must conform to those representations. The exact language of Article 2-313 is as follows.

1. Express warranties by the seller are created as follows:
   a) Any affirmation of fact or promise made by the seller to the buyer which relates to the goods and becomes part of the basis of the bargain creates an express warranty that the goods shall conform to the affirmation or promise.

b) Any description of the goods which is made part of the basis of the bargain creates an express warranty that the goods shall conform to the description.

c) Any sample or model which is made part of the basis of the bargain creates an express warranty that the whole of the goods shall conform to the sample or model.

2. It is not necessary to the creation of an express warranty that the seller use formal words such as "warrant" or "guarantee" or that he have a specific intention to make a warranty, but an affirmation merely of the value of the goods or a statement purporting to be merely the seller's opinion or commendation of the goods does not create a warranty.

One of the problem areas in express warranty cases is in distinguishing between representations which create guarantees and those which are merely "puffing" or "sales talk." For example, in buying a car, most consumers will not take as literal truth the claim by a salesperson that a particular car is "the best on the market." That kind of sales pitch is what the law calls "puffing" or "sales talk." It is not intended to and does not create any guarantee. In contrast, if the salesperson claims a car is brand new when, in fact, it was driven as a demonstrator by the dealership, a guarantee is created. Unfortunately, there are no hard and fast rules which differentiate between "puffery" and guarantees. However, as a general proposition, the more specific the claim, the more likely a court is to find it to be a representation which creates a guarantee. In the final analysis, when in doubt, apply common sense by asking the question: "What would most people understand me to mean by this?"

The Implied Warranty of Fitness for a Particular Purpose as a Product Liability Theory

The implied warranty of fitness for a particular purpose is similar to an express warranty in that the application of the theory does not require a defect in the condition of the product. Like the express warranty theory, the basis of liability is found in that the product fails to conform to the representations made to the buyer. In this case, however, the nature of the representation is narrow and specific. That is, the buyer wanted a product to meet a particular need which was made known to the seller; and the buyer relied on the seller's judgment in selecting the appropriate product. This warranty is found at Article 2-315 of the Uniform Commercial Code and reads as follows.

> Where the seller at the time of contracting has reason to know any particular purpose for which the goods are required and that the buyer is relying on the seller's skill or judgment to select or furnish suitable goods, there is unless excluded or modified under the next section an implied warranty that the goods shall be fit for such purpose.

The plain language of this code section explicitly established two criteria which are critical to the proper application of this warranty. First, the seller must *know of the particular purpose* for which the buyer intends to use the product. Second, the buyer must, in fact, *rely on the seller's skill and judgment* in selecting the product. Like the implied warranty of merchantability, the implied warranty of fitness for a particular purpose may be disclaimed with appropriate language. Disclaimers will be discussed later.

Misrepresentation

As a legal term of art, misrepresentation is a tort for which civil liability attaches. *Black's Law Dictionary* generally defines misrepresentation as: *any manifestation by words or other conduct by one person to another that, under the circumstances, amounts to an assertion not in accordance with the facts.* For the purposes of this discussion, the words misrepresentation, fraud, and deceit can be used interchangeably to refer to the same tort.

In short, misrepresentation is one legal theory under which individuals may be held accountable for their lies. There are five elements to the tort of misrepresentation. Each element must be proven for a plaintiff to prevail. The first element is simply that the defendant made a false representation to the plaintiff. As the definition points out, this falsehood may be perpetrated through words or deeds. The second element is that the defendant knowingly made the false representation. There are three ways in which it can be established that the defendant *knew* the representation to be false. The first is to show that the defendant had actual knowledge that the information was untrue. The second is to show that the defendant made the assertion "without belief in its truth."[1] That is, it is possible to disbelieve something without having actual factual knowledge of its falsehood. Third, knowledge of the falsity of the representation can be shown by proving that the defendant made the assertion with reckless or careless disregard for its truth or falsity.[2] The third element of misrepresentation is that the defendant intended to induce the plaintiff to rely on the false representation. In other words, the defendant wanted the plaintiff to believe the falsehood. The fourth element is that the plaintiff reasonably relied on the representation. This element has two parts. The first is that the plaintiff, in fact, relied on the information. Second, this reliance must have been reasonable. If the representation was completely outrageous or would be deemed to be "puffing" (which was discussed earlier), the plaintiff's reliance is unreasonable and no liability attaches to the defendant. The fifth and final element is damages. Even if each of the first four elements is proven, the defendant has no liability under this theory unless the plaintiff suffered actual losses. Like negligence, it is not enough that damages could have occurred; damages must have occurred before the defendant can be found responsible.

Examples of Misrepresentation Cases

Keith v. Buchanan, Slyman v. Pickwick Farms, and *Gold Kist Peanut Growers Association v. Waldman* illustrate the application of the basic theories to the issues which arise in the various types of misrepresentation cases. *Keith v. Buchanan* analyzes both the express warranty theory and the implied warranty of fitness for a

---

[1]Prosser, William L., *Handbook of the Law of Torts,* 4th ed., St. Paul: West Publishing Co., 1971, p. 699.
    [2]*Ibid.*

particular purpose. The lower court entered judgment for the defendant on both counts. In the appeals court decision which follows, the justices agreed with the trial court that there was no basis for a claim under the implied warranty of fitness for a particular purpose, but did find enough evidence on the express warranty theory.

KEITH v. BUCHANAN
California Court of Appeals, 2nd District, Div. 6
220 Cal.Rptr. 392 (1985)

Facts: Plaintiff, Brian Keith, purchased a sailboat from defendants in November 1978 for a total purchase price of $75,610. Even though plaintiff belonged to the Waikiki Yacht Club, had attended a sailing school, had joined the Coast Guard Auxiliary, and had sailed on many yachts in order to ascertain his preferences, he had not previously owned a yacht. He attended a boat show in Long Beach during October 1978 and looked at a number of boats, speaking to sales representatives and obtaining advertising literature. In the literature, the sailboat which is the subject of this action, called an "Island Trader 41," was described as a seaworthy vessel. In one sales brochure, this vessel is described as "a picture of sure-footed seaworthiness." In another, it is called "a carefully well-equipped, and very seaworthy live-aboard vessel." Plaintiff testified he relied on representations in the sales brochures in regard to the purchase. Plaintiff and a sales representative also discussed plaintiff's desire for a boat which was ocean-going and would cruise long distances.

Plaintiff asked his friend, Buddy Ebsen, who was involved in a boat building enterprise, to inspect the boat. Mr. Ebsen and one of his associates, both of whom had extensive experience with sailboats, observed the boat and advised plaintiff that the vessel would suit his stated needs. A deposit was paid on the boat, a purchase contract was entered into, and optional accessories for the boat were ordered. After delivery of the vessel, a dispute arose in regard to its seaworthiness.

Plaintiff filed the instant lawsuit alleging causes of action in breach of express warranty and breach of implied warranty. The trial court granted defendants'...motion for [summary] judgment at the close of plaintiff's case. The court found that no express warranty was established by the evidence because none of the defendants had undertaken in writing to preserve or maintain the utility or performance of the vessel, nor to provide compensation for any failure in utility or performance. It found that the written statements produced at trial were opinions or commendations of the vessel. The court further found that no implied warranty of fitness was created because the plaintiff did not rely on the skill and judgment of defendants to select and furnish a suitable vessel, but had rather relied on his own experts in selecting the vessel.

Express Warranty: California Uniform Commercial Code section 2313 provides, *inter alia,* that express warranties are created by 1) any affirmation of fact or promise made by the seller to the buyer which relates to the goods and becomes part of the basis of the bargain, and 2) any description of the goods which is made part of the basis of the bargain. Formal words such as "warranty" or "guarantee" are not required to make a warranty, but the seller's affirmation of the value of the goods or an expression of opinion or commendation of the goods does not create an express warranty.

...In deciding whether a statement made by a seller constitutes an express warranty under this provision, the court must deal with three fundamental issues. First, the court must determine whether the seller's statement constitutes an "affirmation of fact or promise" or "description of goods"...or whether it is rather "merely the seller's opinion or commendation of the goods"...Second, assuming the court finds the language used susceptible to creation of a warranty, it must then be determined whether the statement was "part of the basis of the bargain." Third, the court must determine whether the warranty was breached.

A warranty relates to the title, character, quality, identity, or condition of the goods. The purpose of the law of warranty is to determine what it is that the seller has in essence agreed to sell..."Express warranties are chisels in the hands of buyers and sellers. With these tools, the parties to a sale sculpt a monument representing the goods. Having selected a stone, the buyer and seller may leave it almost bare, allowing considerable play in the qualities that fit its contours. Or the parties may chisel away inexactitudes until a well-defined shape emerges. The seller is bound to deliver, and the buyer to accept, goods that match the sculpted form....

A. Affirmation of Fact, Promise, or Description Versus Statement of Opinion, Commendation, or Value

"The determination as to whether a particular statement is an expression of opinion or an affirmation of fact is often difficult, and frequently is dependent upon the facts and circumstances existing at the time the statement is made." ...Recent decisions have evidenced a trend toward narrowing the scope of representations which are considered opinion, sometimes referred to as "puffing" or "sales talk," resulting in an expansion of the liability that flows from broad statements of manufacturers or retailers as to the quality of their products. Courts have liberally construed affirmations of quality made by sellers in favor of injured consumers...It has even been suggested "that in an age of consumerism all seller's statements, except the most blatant sales pitch, may give rise to an express warranty."...

Courts in other States have struggled in efforts to create a formula for distinguishing between affirmations of fact, promises, or descriptions of goods, on the one hand, and value, opinion, or commendation statements, on the other. The code comment indicates that the basic question is: "What statements of the seller have in the circumstances and in objective judgment become part of the basis of the bargain?" The commentators indicated that the language of...the code section was included because "common experience discloses that some statements or predictions cannot fairly be viewed as entering into the bargain."...

Statements made by a seller during the course of negotiation over a contract are presumptively affirmations of fact unless it can be demonstrated that the buyer could only have reasonably considered the statement as a statement of the seller's opinion. Commentators have noted several factors which tend to indicate an opinion statement. These are 1) a lack of specificity in the statement made, 2) a statement that is made in an equivocal manner, of 3) a statement which reveals that the goods are experimental in nature...

It is clear that statements made by a manufacturer or retailer in an advertising brochure which is disseminated to the consuming public in order to induce sales can create express warranties...In the instant case, the vessel purchased was described in sales brochures as "a picture of sure-footed seaworthiness" and "a carefully well-equipped and very sea-worthy vessel." The seller's representative was aware that appellant was looking for a vessel sufficient for long-distance ocean-going cruises. The statements in the brochure are specific and unequivocal in asserting that the vessel is seaworthy. Nothing in the negotiation indicates that the vessel is experimental in nature. In fact, one sales brochure assures prospective buyers that production of the vessel was commenced "after years of careful testing." The representations regarding seaworthiness made in sales brochures regarding the Island Trade 41 were affirmations of fact relating to the quality or condition of the vessel.

B. "Part of the Basis of the Bargain" Test

...California Uniform Commercial Code section 2313 indicates only that the seller's statements must become "part of the basis of the bar-gain."...

...A buyer need not show that he would not have entered into the agreement absent the warranty or even that it was a dominant factor inducing the agreement. A warranty statement is deemed to be part of the basis of the bargain and to have been relied upon as one of the inducements for the purchase of the product. In other words, the buyer's demonstration of reliance on an express warranty is "not a pre-requisite for breach of warranty, as long as the express warranty involved became part of the bargain...If, however, the resulting bargain does not rest at all on the representations of the seller, those representations can-not be considered as becoming any part of the 'basis of the bargain...'"

...The representation need only be part of the basis of the bargain, or merely a factor or consideration inducing the buyer to enter into the bargain. A warranty statement made by a seller is presumptively part of the basis of the bargain, and the burden is on the seller to prove that the resulting bargain does not rest at all on the representation.

The buyer's actual knowledge of the true condition of the goods prior to the making of the contract may make it plain that the seller's statement was not relied upon as one of the inducements for the purchase, but the burden is on the seller to demonstrate such knowledge on the part of the buyer. Where the buyer inspects the goods before purchase, he may be deemed to have waived the seller's express warranties. But an examination or inspection by the buyer of the goods does not necessarily discharge the seller from an express warranty if the defect was not actually discovered and waived...

Appellant's inspection of the boat by his own experts does not constitute a waiver of the express warranty of seaworthiness. Prior to the making of the contract, appellant had experienced boat builders observe the boat, but there was no testing of the vessel in the water. Such a warranty (seaworthiness) necessarily relates to the time when the vessel has been put to sea...and has been shown to be reasonably fit and adequate in materials, construction, and equipment for its intended purposes.

In this case, appellant was aware of the representations regarding seaworthiness by the seller prior to contracting. He also had expressed to the seller's representative his desire for a long-distance ocean-going vessel. Although he had other experts inspect the vessel, the inspection was limited and would not have indicated whether or not the vessel was seaworthy. It is clear that the seller has not overcome the presumption that the representations regarding seaworthiness were part of the basis of the bargain.

Implied Warranty of Fitness for a Particular Purpose: Appellant also claimed breach of the implied warranty of fitness for a particular purpose in regard to the sale of the subject vessel. An implied warranty of fitness for a particular purpose arises when a "seller at the time of contracting has reason to know any particular purpose for which the goods are required and that the buyer is relying on the seller's skill or judgment to select or furnish suitable goods," which are fit for such purpose... The Consumer Warranty Act makes such an implied warranty applicable to retailers, distributors, and manufacturers... An implied warranty of fitness for a particular purpose arises only where 1) the purchaser at the time of contracting intends to use the goods for a particular purpose, 2) the seller at the time of contracting has reason to know of this particular purpose, 3) the buyer relies on the seller's skill or judgment to select or furnish goods suitable for the particular purpose, and 4) the seller at the time of contracting has reason to know that the buyer is relying on such skill and judgment...

The reliance elements are important to the consideration of whether an implied warranty of fitness for a particular purpose exists. "If the seller had no reason to know that he was being relied upon, his conduct in providing goods cannot fairly be deemed a tacit representation of their suitability for a particular purpose. And if the buyer did not in fact rely, then the principal justification for imposing a fitness warranty disappears."... The major question in determining the existence of an implied warranty of fitness for a particular purpose is the reliance by the buyer upon the skill and judgment of the seller to select an article suitable for his needs...

The trial court found that the plaintiff did not rely on the skill and judgment of the defendants to select a suitable vessel, but that he rather relied on his own experts...

A review of the record reveals ample evidence to support the trial court's finding. Appellant had extensive experience with sailboats at the time of the subject purchase, even though he had not previously owned such a vessel. He had developed precise specifications in regard to the type of boat he wanted to purchase. He looked at a number of different vessels, reviewed their advertising literature, and focused on the Island Trader 41 as the object of his intended purchase. He also had friends look at the boat before making the final decision to purchase. The trial court's finding that the buyer did not rely on the skill or judgment of the seller in the selection of the vessel in question is supported by substantial evidence.

The trial court's judgment that no express warranty existed in this matter is reversed. The trial court's judgment is affirmed in all other respects....

Slyman v. Pickwick Farms[3] is a second case involving an alleged breach of an express warranty. The facts of this case, however, present a different problem than that of *Keith*. In this case, Slyman bought a race horse, Masterpoint, from the defendant. At the auction, prior to the opening of the bids on Masterpoint, the following statement was read over the public address system:

This animal at very rare intervals will make a slight noise on expiration of air[.] This is due to the so-called false nasal folds being very slightly more softer than normal[.] The true nasal openings and nasal cavities are normal in size and in no way is the animal's breathing affected[.][4]

This statement was attributed to a veterinarian, Dr. Knappenberger, and was prepared at the request of the defendant. Approximately six months later, Slyman learned that the horse's breathing problems were, in fact, serious and that the horse could not race in such a condition. Subsequently, Slyman sued the defendant claiming a breach of the express warranty created by the statement read at the auction. The basic questions presented in this case are whether a medical opinion can create a warranty, and whether the defendant can be held responsible for a misdiagnosis by a third party professional, the veterinarian. In response to these questions, the court stated as follows:

Of course, whether or not the statement made represents

---

[3]*Slyman v. Pickwick Farms* 472 N.E.2nd 380, Court of Appeals of Ohio, 1984.
[4]*Ibid.*, p. 382.

merely the seller's "puffing" or his opinion and did not form a part of the basis of the bargain between the parties requires that the court consider the circumstances surrounding the sale, the reasonableness of the buyer in believing the seller, and the reliance placed on the seller's statement by the buyer... Here, there is no indication in the record that the plaintiff was equal to or superior in his knowledge of the physical condition of Masterpoint and his respiratory problem than was Knappenberger; nor does the evidence show that he could be expected to have an opinion on the breathing habits of a yearling standard-bred merely from a personal inspection of the horse. However, the record does tend to show that plaintiff did expect to train and run Masterpoint as a standard-bred race horse and, as such, could reasonably have relied upon Knappenberger's statement to indicate that the horse was physically capable of racing. Knappenberger's statements specifically described Masterpoint's respiratory condition and affirmatively stated that "the true nasal openings and nasal cavities are normal in size and in no way is the animal's breathing affected." It could reasonably be concluded that the main purpose behind having this statement read aloud before the sale was to relieve any apprehension or suspicions that might arise as a result of the peculiar sound Masterpoint would occasionally make while breathing, and to convince all those interested in purchasing the horse that it does not have any serious respiratory problems that would affect its racing ability. Thus, Knappenberger's statement was more than just mere opinion or "puffing"; rather, it was a description of Masterpoint's respiratory condition, which, under the circumstances, became a part of the basis of the bargain.

As far as the origin of the statement is concerned, regardless of the fact that the description was formulated by a third party, and not by the seller, the statement may still be found to be part of the basis of the bargain and, therefore, constitutes an express warranty. Nothing in [the applicable statute] requires that the description be made by the seller in order to create an express warranty. "[T]he seller need only introduce it into the bargaining process so that it becomes part of the basis of the bargain.[5]

There is not a plethora of reported product liability cases which have been brought under a theory of the tort of misrepresentation. It appears that this is due to the fact that, as a practical matter, in cases where the facts support a finding of misrepresentation, they also support a breach of warranty claim; and it is easier to prove a breach of warranty (there are fewer elements to prove). One of the few reported cases is that of *Gold Kist Peanut Growers Association v. Waldman.*[6] In this case, Waldman, a farmer, bought peanut seed from Gold Kist. The bags had tags which indicated the seeds tested at 80% for germination. In fact, the seeds tested at 55% for germination. The evidence indicated that germination tests performed prior to the sale of the seed exceeded 80%. However, the quantity of the preservative applied to the seed to prevent it from molding was inadequate. As a result of the mold, the seed subsequently tested at 55% and less. Gold Kist had knowledge of these later tests, but did not change the tags or otherwise inform buyers of the new test results. The court found this evidence to be sufficient to support a finding of fraud against the seed seller.

Although none of these cases directly discusses marketing practices as such, all of them underscore the importance of having marketing and labeling information be consistent with the nature of the product as sold to the consumer. In addition, the last case points out that when new or different information is learned at a later point in time, marketing and labeling information must be corrected to reflect this new information so as not to mislead consumers.

---

[5]*Ibid.*, p. 384.
[6]*Gold Kist Peanut Growers Association v. Waldman,* 377 P.2d 807, Oklahoma, 1962.

Strategies for Protection Against Product Liability Lawsuits

There is a number of strategies which can be employed by engineers, both individually and as part of an organization, to minimize the probability of encountering a product liability lawsuit. If one is sued, these strategies should also assist in defending against the suit and in minimizing the monetary award if one loses. The strategies which will be examined are: the development of legally appropriate inspection and testing procedures, the legally appropriate use of disclaimers and warnings, the development of legally appropriate instructions, and strategies for the individual engineer. The repeated use of "legally appropriate" techniques here is not to be boringly redundant, but to remind the engineer that the legal system uses different standards in evaluating product liability lawsuits than are typically used by engineers in product development and manufacturing. The law's focus on reasonableness, foreseeability, and expectations created by representations must be kept in mind in the product development, manufacture, and marketing processes.

Inspection and Testing Procedures

There are two different perspectives from which engineers should look at inspection and testing procedures. First, tests and inspections are necessary in the design and manufacturing processes to determine if the product performs its intended function. Second, these procedures will assist in the process of determining whether a product is safe.

Before looking at the three kinds of cases (design defect, manufacturing defect, and misrepresentation), there are some general observations which can be made about testing and inspection procedures. Good testing and inspection practices will promote the design and manufacture of high-quality products. This should be a goal of all engineers and manufacturing organizations. Safety is inherent in the creation of high-quality products. As noted earlier, the law does not require products to be perfectly safe. It does, however, require products to be reasonably safe. That is, the probability and magnitude of harm must be balanced against the utility of the product, whether it is possible to make it safer, and if so, the cost of making it safer for users.

Testing and inspection procedures must begin during the design phase of product development. During the design phase, appropriate standards must be selected. That is, applicable governmental or industry standards must be incorporated into the design. That is the minimum. In addition, there are other questions which should be raised. Does the state of the art exceed government and industry standards? Is it wise to incorporate these greater standards even though they are not required? Is it economically feasible? When a design has been completed, the process should commence. If a prototype of the product can be produced, it should be manufactured and tested to determine if the design meets the basic standards of performance, safety, and reliability intended. In other cases, the use of prototypes is not possible. In these cases, techniques such as computer simulations and scale-model testing should be utilized.[7]

In his book, *The Product Liability Handbook: Prevention, Risk, Consequence, and Forensics of Product Failure,* Sam Brown offers a list of twenty-two questions manufacturers should ask design engineers. This check list provides an excellent self-evaluation for the design professional.

DESIGN CHECK LIST

1. Has the product been designed to minimize injury if an accident does occur?

---

[7]Brown, Sam (Ed.), *The Product Liability Handbook: Prevention, Risk, Consequence, and Forensics of Product Failure,* New York: Van Nostrand Reinhold, 1991, p. 69.

2. Has the product been designed for all foreseeable uses? Does the operator require training?

3. Can the product cause an accident?

4. Are warnings located in reasonable place(s) and attached in a reasonable manner so that the consumer will be protected from inherent danger or damage?

5. Are safeguards designed into the product to prevent misuse or removal of the safeguards?

6. Has the product been designed for reliability? How reliable are the predictive methods used; that is, are they experimental or theoretical?

7. Has the environment been considered for all potential applications?

8. Does the product have a "design life?" If the answer is yes, has a mechanism been identified to determine deterioration and decommission of the product before failure?

9. Does the product meet or exceed established guidelines such as governmental statutory codes and regulations, industrial or commercial standards, and national voluntary codes and standards that reflect minimum safety requirements? If the applicable codes conflict, has a ruling or interpretation been requested and has the ruling or interpretation been conveyed to the [appropriate in-house individuals and committees]?

10. Does the company use engineering drawings and related documentation to determine that the dimensions and tolerances meet those specified in standards developed by [appropriate] organizations...? Are the materials properly specified?

11. Are the latest engineering and scientific techniques used to develop and test products?

12. Has rough handling of the product during everyday use and shipping as well as overall wear and tear been considered?

13. Are the instructions for shipping, storage, assembly, installation, operation, and maintenance easy to understand? What will happen if the user does not perform the maintenance procedures?

14. Did the designer review all brochures, catalogs, and other advertising vehicles before they were published?

15. Has product failure been considered in cases where the product is used in conjunction with other components and systems?

16. Can the reliability of the product be improved if a different fabrication process is used?

17. Has the product been assessed for all possible models of failure? Have critical (high-risk) modes of failure been evaluated adequately (in fault-tree, risk, and consequence analyses)?

18. Has the recent technical literature been evaluated with respect to accidents involving users?

19. Was more than one design assessed in a product performance evaluation?

20. Have all loadings (forces, temperature, environmental, etc.) of the product been considered in relation to performance: for example, operation, shop test, *in situ* tests, trans-

portation loads, and emergency, faulted, and accident loads?

21. Has the engineering designer reviewed all data on product failures?

22. Has a lawyer reviewed your quality assurance procedure as a preventive measure?[8]

Appropriate quality assurance procedures are at the heart of lawsuit prevention and damage control at the manufacturing level. At this juncture, the design itself has been subject to scrutiny. Now the scrutiny turns to the manufacturing process.

The first step in ensuring the legal adequacy of the manufacturing process is to ensure that everything is in order to begin manufacturing. While this may sound sophomoric, it must be remembered that the law imposes liability for acts of omission as well as acts of commission. Without detailed systems to force every consideration to be taken into account, unfortunate errors will occur. The following is a check list which can be used for virtually any manufacturing project to ensure against omissions.

MANUFACTURING CHECK LIST
1. Check drawings for proper coordination between trades.

2. Check to make certain that the information on the drawings conforms to that written on the specification(s).

3. Inspect to see that parts, components, structures, and materials conform, specifically and uniquely, to the project.

4. Enter into written agreements with consultants that detail precisely what their responsibilities are.

---

[8]*Ibid.*, pp. 100–101. Reprinted with permission.

5. Review the work performed by consultants for conformity with agreements.

6. Check the final program against the estimate or budget to determine its current validity.

7. Communicate properly with consultants so that a change made by one consultant that affects the work of another is properly accounted for.

8. Include owner–consumers in the communication process to permit them the privilege of determining in advance how their money will be spent.

9. Establish a reasonable time frame for review.

10. Establish a reasonable time for implementation.

11. Specify the schedule, using one of many available network scheduling techniques.

12. Review the specifications to determine whether the items specified are still available or, for that matter, whether they have been available in recent years.

13. Check whether the information given to or by a sales representative or "sales engineer" is valid and conforms to the specification sheet prepared by the company that person represents.

14. Check the bids, quotations, or proposals for conformity with the contract documents.

15. Review the insurance requirements of the contract documents to assure compliance.

16. Review the schedule carefully.

17. Establish and adhere to an orderly system of controlling or keeping track of the documentation that must pass through the manager's hands or office to assure completion of the project.

18. Retain the backup information or supporting data for the approval, modification, or rejection of requests for payment.

19. React in a timely manner to requests for clarification or interpretation of the project documents.

20. Accept the responsibilities that are written into the contract documents.

21. Monitor the progress of the project and report objectively to the owner as required.

22. Assume responsibility for discrepancies and omissions in the project documents.

23. Issue clarifications and instructions that will point out errors on one's part in a timely fashion and thereby eliminate or minimize one's exposure.[9]

Obviously, there are many facets to the manufacturing process. Furthermore, there are ample opportunities for errors resulting in potential legal liability to arise at many different phases of this process. Consequently, it is imperative to have procedures in place with allow for the coordination of the many individuals and departments involved in manufacturing. Beyond employing individual quality assurance personnel, it is important to establish a product liability loss assurance (PLLA) committee whose purpose is to develop a coordinated strategy among all departments toward the end of producing high-quality products.[10] The follow-

---

[9]*Ibid.*, pp. 87–89. Reprinted with permission.
[10]*Ibid.*, p. 89.

ing is a list of thirty-five questions the committee should be prepared to address.

PLLA COMMITTEE CHECK LIST

1. Are the quality assurance manuals up to date?

2. Are records maintained on the testing of product and process?

3. Are guidelines available for ensuring that the committee's mission will be carried out during design, development, production, tests, transportation, handling, operations, maintenance, and repair?

4. Are procedures in place for implementing, updating, and reviewing manuals, instructions, and labels?

5. Is a procedure for packaging and shipping in place?

6. Has a marketing policy or procedure been established?

7. Is a procedure or policy in place for handling customers' complaints or claims?

8. Does the product meet or exceed the standards and/or codes developed by industry associations, technical societies, or government entities?

9. Does the reliability of the product match or exceed that of other, comparable products on the market?

10. Do the instructions, labels, or brochures call the customer and end-user's attention to specific hazards? Do these materials specify the user's responsibilities and obligations for the product?

11. Do the safeguards designed into the product include

misuse or other foreseeable problems? Are the safeguards active or passive?

12. Have adequate steps been taken to prevent the inherent dangers of the product to company employees as well as customers?

13. Have steps been taken to monitor outside suppliers of components or parts to ensure that the product containing those components or parts will be safe?

14. Has the company conducted every reasonable test to assure the safety of the product?

15. Do the records reflect the company's safety endeavors?

16. Are databases on product performance available from industry associations, technical societies, user associations, and governmental agencies? Is this information used to remedy problems in as expeditious a manner as possible?

17. Have consequence and risk analyses been performed? What is the worst possible consequence that can be the result of the worst possible defect (based on current inspection methods and the safety features already built in)?

18. Has the committee recommended preventative or protective measures to eliminate or control hazards?

19. Have all operating and faulted (emergency, runaway, scram) reactions caused by operator or equipment malfunction been identified in fault-tree, risk, and consequence analyses? Does the equipment have proprietary or specialized uses? Has the user supplied performance requirements? Have these requirements been specified contractually and reviewed by the committee's engineering and legal representatives?

20. Have the histories of hazards, failures, and mishaps of existing systems been reviewed?

21. Does the committee keep management informed about its status, significant problems, deficiencies, and methods of improvement?

22. Does the committee participate in design preparations and reviews to ensure that incompatible or unsafe design, process, operation, and maintenance procedures are not incorporated?

23. Does the committee participate in product performance ratings to ensure that safety is not compromised by changes in mission, hardware, configuration, procedures, and the like?

24. Does the company have an independent review procedure or audit for each major function in the company, including the PLLA committee.

25. Does the committee monitor reports of failures and incidents to determine the presence of discrepancies, deficiencies, or trends that might affect safety? Does it make suitable recommendations for corrective action?

26. Does the committee ensure that safety training programs are adequate to meet organizational needs? Does it initiate improvements for such training?

27. Does the committee investigate mishaps involving the product while the product is the company's responsibility?

28. Has the committee developed a plan for investigating mishaps involving the product?

29. Do the members of the PLLA committee serve on

boards or committees that deal with industrial safety or related areas?

30. Are protective equipment, warning devices, and emergency and rescue equipment required for the product? Is that equipment selected and properly identified?

31. Has information on hazards been disseminated through other organizations that might be affected?

32. Have corrective actions been taken to prevent the recurrence of mishaps caused by similar deficiencies or practices?

33. Have the effects on product safety of outside suppliers been determined?

34. Is a mechanism in place for preparing safety analysis programs required by customers or clients?

35. Does a mechanism exist for analyzing safety requirements, procedures, and milestones required by subcontractors?[11]

The strategies for preventing misrepresentation cases have already been incorporated in the various check lists. Remember that misrepresentation cases involve a false representation concerning the product. The primary method by which such representations can be prevented is by having the appropriate engineers and quality assurance personnel review all relevant paper work which relates to the marketing of the product to ensure there is no misinformation contained therein. The materials which should be reviewed include such things as: brochures, instructions, labels, warnings, catalog descriptions, and packaging materials (looking for misleading pictures and the like). Most organizations live with a certain amount of the right hand not know-

---

[11]*Ibid.,* pp. 91–93. Reprinted with permission.

ing what the left hand is doing. From the standpoint of product liability litigation, that is a bomb waiting to go off. Coordinated efforts are critical to product performance, reliability, and safety.

Use of Disclaimers

The Uniform Commercial Code permits the disclaimer of its warranties under some circumstances. Generally, it is most difficult to disclaim an express warranty; and it is the easiest to disclaim the implied warranty of merchantability. The implied warranty of fitness for a particular purpose is somewhere in between the two. The explicit provision regulating disclaimers is found at Article 2-316.

(1) Words or conduct relevant to the creation of an express warranty and words or conduct tending to negate or limit warranty shall be construed wherever reasonable as consistent with each other; but subject to the provisions of this Article on parol or extrinsic evidence...negation or limitation is inoperative to the extent that such construction is unreasonable.

(2) Subject to subsection (3), to exclude or modify the implied warranty of merchantability or any part of it the language must mention merchantability and in case of a writing must be conspicuous, and to exclude or modify any implied warranty of fitness the exclusion must be by a writing and conspicuous. Language to exclude all implied warranties of fitness is sufficient if it states, for example, that "There are no warranties which extend beyond the description on the face hereof."

(3) Notwithstanding subsection (2)
(a) unless the circumstances indicate otherwise, all implied warranties are excluded by expressions like "as is," "with all faults" or other language which in common understanding

calls the buyer's attention to the exclusion of warranties and makes plain that there is no implied warranty; and

(b) when the buyer before entering into the contract has examined the goods or the sample or model as fully as he desired or has refused to examine the goods there is no implied warranty with regard to defects which an examination ought in the circumstances to have revealed to him; and

(c) an implied warranty can also be excluded or modified by course of dealing or course of performance or usage of trade.

There are three foci to determining the legal sufficiency of a disclaimer. First, is the language of the disclaimer consistent or inconsistent with the language of the warranty purportedly given? Second, was the disclaimer put in writing? Third, was the written disclaimer conspicuous (as opposed to, for example, being hidden in the small print)?

O'Neil v. International Harvester Company is an example of a case which, among other things, examines the use of a disclaimer under the theories of express warranty and the implied warranty of fitness for a particular purpose. O'Neil's case was dismissed by the trial judge. At this point, he is appealing that dismissal.

O'NEIL v. INTERNATIONAL HARVESTER COMPANY
Colorado Court of Appeals
575 P.2d 862 (1978)

Facts: ...On August 22, 1975, O'Neil entered into a "Retail Installment Contract" with the defendant, International Harvester Company, for the purchase of a used diesel tractor and trailer. International Harvester Company assigned its interest in the contract to the defendant, International Harvester Credit Corporation. The contract provided, *inter alia:*

> Each USED motor vehicle covered by this contract is sold AS IS WITHOUT ANY WARRANTY OF ANY CHARACTER, expressed or implied, unless purchaser has received from seller a separate written warranty executed by seller.

No written warranties were received by O'Neil. The contract also provided:

> Purchaser agrees that this contract...which he has read and to which he agrees contains the entire agreement relating to the installment sale of said property and supersedes all previous contracts and agreements between purchaser and seller relating to the order of sale of said property except as to any written agreements between purchaser and seller concerning warranty.

Pursuant to the contract, O'Neil paid $1,700 as a down payment, but failed to make any of the required monthly payments.

According to O'Neil's deposition, shortly after the purchase, his employee drove the truck to a location in the mountains for the purpose of hauling firewood to Denver. He had numerous problems with the truck, causing delays which resulted in the loss of his permit to cut and remove firewood, as well as loss of business. A representative of International Harvester agreed to pay one-half of the cost of certain repairs. After several attempts to have the defendants repair the truck during the next month, O'Neil returned it to the defendants, but the defendants refused to rescind the sale.

O'Neil admitted reading the contract, including the warranty exclusion provision. He stated, however, that he understood the provision to mean that the tractor and trailer would be in the condition represented by the defendant's salesman. According to O'Neil, the salesman represented that the truck had been recently overhauled and would be suitable for operation in the mountains; later, when he returned the truck, O'Neil overheard another employee of the defendant International Harvester Company say to the salesman, *inter alia,* "I told you not to sell him Inman's truck—Inman took every piece of used equipment off his other fleet of trucks and stuck it on that one."

In his complain, O'Neil sought both recision of the contract and damages, alleging that International Harvester was liable for breach of express warranties, [and] an implied warranty fitness for a particular purpose...

Disclaimer of Warranties: Pursuant to the Uniform Commercial Code, one way an implied warranty of fitness for a particular purpose can be excluded is by a conspicuous writing which states generally that there are no warranties extending beyond the description in the contract...O'Neil admits reading the warranty disclaimer provision. Thus, we need not decide whether as a matter of law it was "conspicuous."...And we hold that as the language "as is without warranty of any character expressed or implied" was sufficient to inform O'Neil that there was no implied warranty in effect for the truck...

Even though express warranties are also included in the above-quoted language, still O'Neil asserts that [the dismissal] was improvidently granted against him on his claim that International Harvester breached the express warranties. The defendants argue that the trial court's ruling was correct. We agree with O'Neil.

Section 4-2-316,..., provides that "[w]ords or conduct relevant to the creation of an express warranty *and* words or conduct tending to negate or limit warranty shall be construed wherever reasonable as consistent with each other..." (emphasis added). Here, the oral warranties relied upon by O'Neil are totally inconsistent with the warranty exclusion clause of the contract. Section 4-2-316 further provides that, under these circumstances (but subject to the provisions of the Code governing the admission of parol evidence), a provision limiting an express warranty is inoperative.

Turning to the applicable parol evidence rule...one finds that:

Terms with respect to which the confirmatory memoranda of the parties agree or which are otherwise set forth in writing intended by the parties as a final expression of their agreement with respect to such terms as are included therein, may not be contradicted by evidence of any prior agreement or of a contemporaneous oral agreement...

Various commentators have noted the difficulty in applying [these sections] when, as here, the buyer alleges oral warranties by the seller, but the written contract contains both a warranty disclaimer clause and an "integration" provision...While the courts divide on whether testimony as to the oral warranties may be admitted under these circumstances,..., we do not reach that issue in this case.

Where, as here, the buyer alleges the existence of oral warranties prior to execution of the written contract, as well as conduct following the sale (such as a commitment to pay for certain repairs) which tends to show that warranties were in fact made, there is a material issue of fact for resolution. That issue is whether the parties intended the written contract to be a final expression of their agreement and, if not, what the terms actually agreed upon by the parties consisted of. Further, we hold that, under such circumstances, evidence of both oral warranties and the conduct of the parties subsequent to signing the contract is admissible for the purpose of resolving this issue. Thus, entry of summary judgment on this issue was in error...

Duty to Warn

Products which are otherwise dangerous to users can, in many instances, be made safe with the provision of appropriate warnings. In cases where there are no warnings, or the warnings given are alleged to be inadequate, the legal theories a plaintiff's attorney will look to are strict liability and negligence. Under a strict liability claim, the plaintiff alleges the lack of (or inadequate) warnings made the product "unreasonably dangerous." In negligence cases, the claim is that a "reasonable and prudent person" would have provided warnings or more adequate warnings. Regardless of the theory selected, there are three things a plaintiff must prove in a duty to warn case: "1. a duty to warn existed, 2. that no warning was given or the warning given was inadequate and 3. that the injury sustained was caused by the lack or inadequacy of a warning."[12]

In determining whether a duty to warn existed, there are three critical factors: 1) the probability of an injury resulting from a foreseeable use of the product, 2) the likely magnitude of the injury, and 3) the feasibility of issuing a warning. Once it has been determined that a warning is appropriate, the courts have established the legal standards by which its adequacy will be evaluated.

1. The warning must be in a form that would be reasonably expected to catch the attention of a reasonably prudent person under the circumstances of use.

2. The content of the warning must be comprehensible to a reasonable person and must convey the nature and extent of the danger.

3. It is implied in the duty to warn that there is a duty to warn with a degree of intensity that would cause a reasonable person to exercise caution commensurate with the potential danger.[13]

Generally speaking, guidance can be found in simply remembering that the purpose of the warning is to compel the user to behave differently so as to avoid injury. With this in mind, the question becomes: does this warning accomplish this purpose?

As a factual matter, the circumstances under which a duty to warn arises can be summarized into six types of situations. First, machines which are hazardous to operate must possess appropriate warnings. Second, warnings must be given to consumer products which are inherently dangerous through either use or misuse.

---

[12]Hall, Gerald, *The Failure to Warn Handbook,* Columbia, MD: Hanrow Press, Inc., 1986, p. 1.
[13]*Ibid.,* p. 2. Reprinted with permission.

Third, physical structures with dangerous features (e.g., stairs without a handrail) must have warnings. Fourth, warnings must be provided with naturally occurring physical conditions (e.g., a swimming hole). Fifth, physical conditions caused by human conduct (e.g., a slippery floor) must contain posted warnings. And sixth, physical conditions which have been made dangerous by nature (e.g., ice or snow) must contain appropriate warnings.[14]

In assessing a particular situation to determine whether it is appropriate for warnings (and, if so, what warnings), there are twelve factors which should be assessed.

1. The scope of the product's uses.

2. The environments in which the product will be used.

3. The user population.

4. All possible hazards.

5. The probability of the occurrence of specific hazards.

6. The nature and seriousness of the possible personal injuries.

7. The nature of alternative design features, including warnings and instructions, which will mitigate or eliminate the hazard(s).

8. The nature of other hazards created by the alternative design features.

9. Whether the alternative design features affect the usefulness of the product.

10. The cost of the alternative design features.

---

[14]*Ibid.*, p. 2.

11. This product compared to similar products.

12. Tested warnings and/or instructions to determine whether users will follow them.[15]

Hagans v. Oliver Machinery Co. is one of the cases discussed earlier in relation to the problem of negligent design as a product liability theory. Two other theories argued in that case related to the duty to warn. *Hagans* is the case in which the plaintiff was injured when using a saw after the blade guard assembly had been removed. The essence of the duty to warn portion of the case was the claim that the defendant violated both strict liability and negligence law by failing to provide a warning about the dangers of using the saw after removing the guard. The following is what the court had to say in reference to each theory.

HAGANS v. OLIVER MACHINERY CO.
U.S. Court of Appeals (5th Circuit)
576 F.2d 97 (1978)

Failure to Warn—Strict Liability Theory: A product is unreasonably dangerous and, therefore, defective if the ordinary man knowing the risks and dangers involved in its use would not have marketed the product without 'supplying warnings as to the risks and dangers involved in using the product as well as instructions as to how to avoid those risks and dangers.'

.   .   .

Plaintiff argues that defendant's failure to warn users of the risks involved in operating the saw without the blade guard assembly rendered the saw unreasonably dangerous. A conspicuous warning plate

---

[15] Weinstein, Aven; Twerski, Aaron D.; Piehler, Henry R.; and Donaher, William A., *Products Liability and the Reasonably Safe Product*, New York, John Wiley & Sons, Inc., 1978.

permanently attached to the machine would have sufficed, according to plaintiff.

The rule requiring manufacturers to inform users of the risks inherent in their products is based on the sound policy that the user is entitled to the information necessary to make an intelligent choice as to whether the product's utility or benefits justify exposing himself to the risk of harm...Implicit, therefore, in the duty to warn is the requirement that the user be ignorant of the dangers warned against...Thus, it is generally held that there is no duty to warn when the danger or potentiality of danger is obvious or is actually known to the injured person...

One can imagine no more obvious danger than that posed by the jagged edge of a circular saw blade spinning at 3600 revolutions per minute. Moreover, plaintiff admitted that he was aware of the dangers involved in cutting knotted wood on the saw. Clearly, a warning of the dangers involved in using the saw would not have informed him of anything he did not already know.

Plaintiff also contends that defendant should have provided a warning informing users of the existence of the removable blade guard assembly. This Court rejected an identical contention in *Ward v. Hobart Mfg. Co.,...,*commenting: "It seems superfluous to require a manufacturer to warn a user of the danger of using a machine without a safety device where the user is fully conscious of such danger in the absence of the safety device." Although *Ward* was a negligence case, we find its reasoning equally applicable to a claim that lack of such warning constitutes an unreasonably dangerous defect...

Failure to Warn—Negligence Theory: The universally recognized duty of a manufacturer to warn of dangers associated with the use of his product does not attach, according to the great weight of authority, when the danger is "open and obvious" or the party to be warned is already aware of the danger...

As we concluded earlier, the danger posed by defendant's product was not only obvious but was known to and appreciated by plaintiff. We have likewise previously disposed of plaintiff's contention that the saw should have carried a warning that informed users of the existence of a blade guard attachment.

Duty to Provide Instructions

As has been previously pointed out, one of the techniques for turning an unsafe product into a legally safe one is to provide adequate instructions. The basis for determining the need for and nature of the instructions is essentially the same analysis previously discussed in relation to warnings. If the provision of instructions is sufficient to render the product reasonably safe for reasonably foreseeable uses and misuses, then there is a legal obligation to provide them. Like warnings, instructions must be adequate. Again, it is important for the engineering professionals, the quality assurance professionals, and the marketing professionals to work cooperatively in these areas to ensure the most legal protection through the development of the most appropriate warnings and instructions.

Protection from Liability for Individual Engineers

Circumstances can arise under which individual engineers may find themselves as named defendants in product liability lawsuits. While performing at the highest levels of professional competence reduces the probability of becoming involved in litigation, there are no guarantees. For those engineers who work for companies, particularly large ones, the probability of being a named defendant is the most remote. The assets of the business will far outweigh those of the individual engineer. Consequently, few attorneys will attempt to pursue the individual—it is not worth the time or energy. However, engineers who work on their own or for smaller companies with fewer assets are more susceptible to the probability of being sued. The following strategies should be considered carefully for their appropriateness to individual circumstances. In some cases, professional advice should be sought from an experienced attorney or insurance agent.

Company Policy—The first place to look for protection is from your company. What is your company's policy when a product liability lawsuit is filed? Will the company cover the legal fees of engineers named in the lawsuit? What is covered by the company's insurance policy? Does your company employ procedures and standards which are designed to create and produce reliable and safe products?

Insurance—Individual engineers who are self-employed or who work for companies which do not offer protection to their employees should consider acquiring errors and omissions insurance. This is particularly important for design engineers.

Going Bare—This refers to the strategy of choosing to carry no insurance. It is typically coupled with a strategy of owning nothing of any value in one's name. For example, a married engineer may "own" a house, but the deed is in the spouse's name only. While this can be a good strategy, it must be weighed against the problems it may create if the marriage ends in a divorce.

Incorporation—A self-employed engineer or small business which is not incorporated should consider incorporation as a strategy. Once the business is incorporated, for the purposes of lawsuits (among other things), the corporation is an entity which is separate and distinct from its owners. As a practical matter, little changes in the day-to-day operations of the business, but the engineer is now an employee of the corporation.

Defenses to Product Liability Lawsuits

There are a number of defenses available to defendants in product liability lawsuits. In this context, the word "defense" refers to a legal theory by which the defendant will shift the responsibility, in total or in part, to the plaintiff. Another way to think of it is that the defendant is saying: "Even if I did what you say I did, you are (partially or completely) responsible for your own injuries because your conduct violated the law too." (Note that this is different from a defendant saying: "I did not do it, someone harmed you, but it was not me" or "I did everything you say I did, but it is not a violation of the law.") There are four defenses which will be discussed here: contributory negligence, comparative negligence, assumption of the risk, and the state-of-the-art defense.

Contributory Negligence

The phrase "contributory negligence" has two meanings: one as the name of a legal theory, and a second as the description of a plaintiff's conduct. In its descriptive sense, contributory negligence refers to negligent conduct on the part of the plaintiff which is a contributing cause to his or her injuries. In this sense, the phrase is used in conjunction with other defense theories such as comparative negligence.

As a legal theory, once the defendant proves the plaintiff was contributorily negligent, the plaintiff loses the lawsuit. That is, it acts as a complete bar to the plaintiff recovering anything from the defendant regardless of their relative proportions of fault for the incident. Historically, the theory of contributory negligence evolved to correct the injustice created by situations where both the plaintiff and defendant were partially responsible for the injuries. Prior to its evolution, the plaintiff's negligence had no bearing on the outcome. If the defendant was negligent, the defendant was found responsible for the entire value of the damages. However, while contributory negligence corrected this injustice, it created another one. That is, under the contributory negligence theory, the plaintiff loses everything even if his or her contributing negligence was minuscule in comparison to the defendant's negligence. To address this inequity, two other theories have evolved which attempt to strike a more reasonable balance in situations where both the plaintiff and defendant are partially responsible for the damage: comparative negligence and assumption of the risk. As a result of the evolution of these new theories, contributory negligence has virtually disappeared as a legal theory, but the phrase continues to be used in its descriptive sense.

Comparative Negligence

Comparative negligence is a legal theory applied in negligence cases which places liability for the economic loss suffered by the plaintiff on each of the parties in proportion to their fault. There are two types of comparative negligence: pure comparative negligence and partial comparative negligence. Pure comparative negligence imposes responsibility strictly according to the proportion of fault assessed against each party. For example, if a plaintiff is found 10% at fault and the defendant is found 90% at fault, the plaintiff will collect 90% of the value of damages from the defendant. Conversely, if the plaintiff is found 90% at fault and the defendant is found to be only 10% at fault, the plaintiff will collect 10% of the value of damages from the defendant.

Most States do not follow the rule of pure comparative negligence, but instead use the rule of partial comparative negligence. Under the rule of partial comparative negligence, the plaintiff will recover damages based on the defendant's proportion of fault *but only if* the defendant is found to be more at fault than the plaintiff. Consequently, in the previous example where the plaintiff was found to be 90% at fault and the defendant was found to be

10% at fault, the plaintiff would not be entitled to any damages from the defendant under a partial comparative negligence theory.

Colter v. Barber-Greene Company & Another is an example of the application of comparative negligence principles to a product liability lawsuit alleging violations of warranty and negligence law. In this case, the court presents the arguments for allowing contributory negligence to reduce a negligence award, for contributory negligence not reducing a breach of warranty recovery, and for product misuse barring recovery under a breach of warranty theory.

COLTER v. BARBER-GREENE COMPANY & ANOTHER

Massachusetts S.J.C.

403 Mass. 50 (1988)

Statement of Proceedings Prior to this Appeal: On December 5, 1978, David E. Colter suffered severe arm injuries while greasing the gears of a twin screw sand classifier owned and operated by Colter's employer, Marshfield Sand & Gravel Company (Marshfield). The machine was manufactured by a division of the Barber-Greene Company (Barber-Greene) which sold it to Worcester Sand & Gravel Company (Worcester). Worcester traded the machine to New England Road Machinery Company (New England), which later sold it to Marshfield. Colter sued Barber-Greene, Worcester, and New England asserting causes of action for negligence, breach of implied warranty of merchantability, and breach of implied warranty of fitness for a particular use. The jury found Barber-Greene to have been 36% negligent, found New England to have been 15% negligent, found Worcester not to have been negligent, and found Colter to have been 49% contributorily negligent. On the warranty count, the jury found that Barber-Greene and New England each had breached its implied warranty of merchantability and had proximately caused Colter's injuries. However, the jury also found that Colter's recovery was barred because he had no knowledge of the machine's defective condition, but nonetheless proceeded unreasonably to use the machine.

Barber-Greene and New England moved for judgment notwithstanding the verdict or for a new trial, arguing that the finding on the warranty count was inconsistent with and negated the finding that Barber-Greene's and New England's negligence proximately caused Colter's injuries. The trial judge ruled that New England and Barber-Greene were entitled to judgment in their favor. Colter subsequently filed a motion for relief from judgment on the basis of *Richard v. American Mfg. Co.*....The judge allowed the motion and entered judgment for Colter. New England and Barber-Greene appealed. This court granted Barber-Greene's application for direct appellate review. We conclude that there is sufficient evidence on the issue whether the negligent design of the sand classifier proximately caused Colter's injuries to submit that claim to the jurors. We agree with Barber-Greene that the evidence on negligent failure to warn is insufficient. Because the jurors were not asked to apportion Colter's negligence between the two theories of negligence, there must be a new trial on negligent design.

Facts: At the time of his accident, Colter was employed as a manager at Marshfield's quarry in Weymouth. Marshfield operated quarrying equipment as this location including the twin screw classifier which consisted of a rectangular hopper containing two screw augers. The screws were driven by a set of bevel gears which ran at a speed of approximately twenty to thirty revolutions per minute. The gears, which were powered by an electric motor, were mounted on a steel frame approximately twenty feet above ground. A conveyor belt fed wet sand into the hopper. The screws carried the sand upward to another conveyor belt. The action of the screws removed the water from the sand; the water poured out the low end of the machine.

Barber-Greene's specifications called for a guard to cover the bevel gears, and they did not sell the machine without one. When Worcester purchased the machine involved in Colter's accident in 1952, the purchase included a bevel gear guard. By the time New England took the twin screw sand classifier from Worcester in trade, there was no guard on the machine and the owner's manual which showed the guard in place was missing as well. New England sold the machine to Marshfield in 1969 without the guard or the owner's manual. New England did not inform Marshfield that the machine's bevel gears should be covered. Although Barber-Greene manufactured replacement guards, Marshfield never obtained a guard for the gears.

Colter began his employment with Marshfield in 1971 as a concrete salesman assigned to Marshfield's Cohasset office. In 1975, Colter was promoted to the position of safety director at the Weymouth plant. In the summer of 1977, Marshfield moved the sand classifier to Weymouth and mounted it on the twenty-foot high steel structure. Although Colter was generally aware of the dangers of exposed gears, he was not aware that the machine required a guard. Personnel from the United States Bureau of Mine Safety and Health Administration frequently inspected the Weymouth facility, but never instructed Colter to obtain a bevel gear guard for the sand classifier because the gear box was mounted above ground.

On the day of the accident, Colter arrived at work sometime between 10:30 and 11:00 a.m. The plant's operation had started late that day because the cold weather had frozen some pipes. Shortly after lunch, Colter passed the "wet end of the plant" and heard a loud screaming "steel-on-steel" noise emanating from the gears of the sand classifier. Colter had never heard the machine make this kind of noise and, because the noise was so loud, he feared that the machine would come apart. Colter knew that the company's operations at that time were critical, and that, if the sand classifier broke, it would put Marshfield's client out of business. Responding to what he believed to be an emergency situation, Colter instructed another employee [to] get him a grease gun. After obtaining the grease gun, Colter drove a front-end loader to the steel structure supporting the sand classifier. Colter climbed onto the structure, and stood in the middle of the conveyor belt on two angle irons. He injected grease into the gears on one side and the noise stopped. Before Colter descended from the machine, his jacket caught in the gears, pulling in his arms. Colter suffered severe injuries requiring the amputation of his right arm below the elbow, amputation of his left index finger, and causing substantial loss of function in his left arm.

Negligent Design: Barber-Greene contends that the judge denied erroneously its motion for a directed verdict on the negligence counts....

On the issue of negligent design, Colter alleged that the design of the twin screw classifier was defective in two major respects. First, Colter argued that the sand classifier was defectively designed because it used outdated power transmission elements which required manual greasing rather than using fully enclosed elements which rotated in their own lubricating bath. The latter design eliminated the need to guard against injury from greasing the gears because the gears were self-lubricating. Given that the machine involved in Colter's accident used exposed power transmission elements, Colter argued that the sand classifier was deficient in a second respect, namely, that the guard that covered the exposed gears was improperly designed. Colter argued that the gear guard was defective because it contained large openings that would allow sand and dirt to enter the gears thus ensuring that the guard would need frequent removal for cleaning, greasing, and other mainte-nance. Colter also argued that the gear guard was too cumbersome to be removed and replaced easily and that the guard, by its own improper design, invited permanent removal.

Colter presented the expert testimony of Egor Paul, a professor of mechanical engineering, who stated that the sand classifier itself was defectively designed because the power transmission elements were exposed to the dirty, sandy environment of the gravel yard and thus required frequent cleaning and greasing. Paul stated that designs which fully enclosed the power transmission elements in a self-lubricating bath had been available since the 1930's, and that these designs eliminated the need for greasing the transmission elements.

Paul's testimony was corroborated by Ameilio Salera, the president of New England Road Machinery Co., who stated that his company did not manufacture and sell open-gear sand classifiers because the company considered the closed-gear model to be more safe. Salera stated that he considered the enclosed gear design to be safer because it reduced the number of times any worker risked contact with exposed gears. James Mueller, manager of marketing services for Barber-Greene, stated that Barber-Greene manufactured sand classifiers with enclosed gearboxes in the 1950's, and that one of the reasons for the enclosed design related to safety concerns.

As regards the gear guard itself, Colter contended that the guard was defective because the gear guard did not completely enclose the gears, but left an opening at the bottom and two additional cutouts in the guard. Professor Paul testified that because the machine was intended for use in a sandy, dusty environment, the openings guaranteed that the gears would need frequent greasing. James Mueller stated that Barber-Greene expected that the sand classifier's gear guard could need to be removed twice a month so that the machine could be washed, greased, and serviced. Although Worcester's representative stated that he did not know what happened to the gear guard, on cross-examination Barber-Greene's representative recognized that the sand classifier's gears might need washing as many as 624 times between the machine's manufacture in 1952 and Colter's accident in 1978. Worcester's representative, Matteo Trotto, testified that the gears never were washed and repaired. Trotto stated that he did not know whether the guard was removed for the greasing, but that the repairs possibly would have required the guard's removal.

Because the guard would need to be removed frequently, Colter argued that the guard was negligently designed because it was not easily removed and replaced. The gear guard designed by Barber-Greene weighed approximately sixty pounds and was attached to the sand classifier by five bolts. Two workers were required to remove and replace the guard. The gears were mounted on the high end of the machine, and Barber-Greene acknowledged that the gears could be mounted as high as forty feet off the ground. Professor Paul stated that a proper design would have included a hinged opening or access panels which would have allowed a worker to grease the gears without removing the guard. The plaintiff's expert testified that design considerations appropriately account for the frequency of removal. Barber-Greene never tested the guard to determine the ease of removal.

We hold a manufacturer liable for defectively designed products because the manufacturer is in the best position to recognize and eliminate the design defects..."In evaluating the adequacy of a product's design, the jury should consider, among other factors, 'the gravity of the danger posed by the challenged design, the likelihood that such danger would occur, the mechanical feasibility of a safer alternative design, the financial cost of an improved design, and the adverse consequences to the product and to the consumer that would result from an alternative design.'"..."[T]here is a case for the jury if the plaintiff can show an available design modification which would reduce the risk without undue cost or interference with the performance of the machinery." As the Appeals Court has noted, it is the jury's function to determine "whether the circumstances of the guard's removal and the plaintiff's subsequent injury were reasonably foreseeable."...

Based on the evidence, the jury was entitled to find that Barber-Greene had negligently designed the twin screw sand classifier. The jury could have found that the open gear design was defective because it allowed sand and dirt to enter the machinery, thus necessitating frequent cleanings and greasings. The jury could have found that the enclosed gear design provided a safer alternative to the open-gear sand classifier. The evidence was undisputed that Barber-Greene manufactured an enclosed gear sand classifier in 1952, and Barber-Greene's representative could not say which design was more expensive.

The jury also could have found that the open guard was defective as well. Moreover, the jury could have found that, because the guard lacked any access panels or doors through which an individual could clean or grease the gears, the guard had to be removed each time the bevel gears required attention. Because the gear guard was so cumbersome, the jury could have concluded that it was entirely foreseeable that a purchaser of the machine would remove the guard permanently. In the absence of any testimony as to what actually happened to the gear guard while the sand classifier was in Worcester's possession, the jury was entitled to infer that the guard was removed for greasing and repair and was not replaced because it was too cumbersome, not efficient, and too costly in the labor required to remove and replace.

Negligent Failure to Warn: On the issue of its negligent failure to warn of the hazards of cleaning the bevel gears without shutting down the machine's operation, Barber-Greene contends that Colter's admitted knowledge of the dangers inherent in greasing the machine without the guard relieves the company of liability because Barber-Greene's failure to warn was not the proximate cause of Colter's injuries. As this court has recognized, where danger presented by a given product is obvious, no duty to warn may be required because a warning will not reduce the likelihood of injury...Colter admitted he knew it was dangerous to grease gears while operating the machine. In these circumstances, a warning would not reduce the likelihood of injury. We therefore agree with Barber-Greene that it was entitled to a judgment on this theory as a matter of law.

Breach of Warranty: On the warranty count, the jury found that Barber-Greene had breached its warranty of merchantability with respect to the design, manufacture, and sale of the sand classifier, and that New England had breached its warranty of merchantability with respect to the sale of the machine. The jury found that the defendants' breaches had proximately caused Colter's injuries, but found that Colter had actual knowledge of the defective condition of the sand classifier, and that he had proceeded unreasonably to use the machine, thus injuring himself. This finding precluded Colter's recovery on the warranty count. As explicated in this court's decision in *Correia v. Firestone Tire & Rubber Co.,...,* a plaintiff's knowing and unreasonable use of a defective product is an affirmative defense to a defendant's breach of warranty...Barber-Greene and New England contend that the jury's affirmative answer to a question on unreasonable use on the warranty count also relieves them from negligence liability because, for both counts, Colter's own conduct was the proximate cause of his injuries. We do not agree.

Plaintiff's Contributory Negligence: Barber-Greene and New England principally rely on language in *Correia* to support their contention that Colter's unreasonable use of the sand classifier is, for purposes of negligence, a bar to recovery. This court stated: "The user's negligence does not prevent recovery except when he unreasonably uses a product that he knows to be defective and dangerous. In such circumstances, the user's conduct alone is the proximate cause of his injuries, as a matter of law, and recovery is appropriately denied. In short, the user is denied recovery, not because of his contributory negligence or his assumption of the risk but rather because his conduct is the proximate cause of his injuries."...

Although there is a certain logic to the defendants' argument that a finding of unreasonable use in a warranty count negates a finding of proximate cause on a negligence count, the argument is flawed because it equates proximate cause with sole cause. An examination of the principles underlying liability in negligence and liability in warranty indicates that, while sole proximate cause is a component of the warranty inquiry, negligence liability does not focus on a sole cause of the plaintiff's injuries.

It is a well-settled proposition that actions for negligence and for breach of warranty impose distinct duties and standards of care. The basic elements of a product liability action founded on negligence are duty, breach of duty, cause in fact, and proximate cause...The focus of the negligence inquiry is on the conduct of the defendant. We impose liability when a product's manufacturer or seller has failed to use reasonable care to eliminate foreseeable dangers which subject a user to an unreasonable risk of injury...."[A] finding of negligence [is] a statement by the jury about the product and about the manufacturer as well. It signifie[s] that the product was unreasonably dangerous because of its design or because of its failure to be accompanied by an adequate warning, or both. It also signifie[s] that an ordinarily prudent manufacturer would have recognized the product's shortcomings and would have taken appropriate corrective measures."...

Liability for breach of warranty stands on a much different footing. In Massachusetts, liability for breach of warranty of merchantability is governed by G.L.c. 106, sections 2-314–2-318 (1986 ed.), and this court has noted that these provisions are congruent, in all material respects, with the principles expressed in Restatement (Second) of Torts Section 402A (1965), the Restatement's definition of a seller's strict liability for harm suffered by a user or consumer of a seller's product...Unlike negligence liability, warranty liability "focuses on whether the product was defective and unreasonably dangerous and not on the conduct of the user or the seller."...Because a breach of warranty does not require a defendant's misconduct, a defendant may be liable on a theory of breach of warranty of merchantability even though he or she properly designed, manufactured, and sold his or her product...Clearly, liability based on a theory of strict liability differs significantly from liability based on negligence. "A defendant in a products liability case in this Commonwealth may be found to have breached its warranty of merchantability without having been negligent, but the reverse is not true. A defendant cannot be found to have been negligent without having breached the warranty of merchantability."

In a negligence case, the conduct of the plaintiff which will serve to bar recovery is governed by statute. Our comparative negligence statute provides that the plaintiff's contributory negligence shall not bar recovery if the plaintiff's negligence was not greater than the total amount of negligence attributable to the parties against whom recovery is sought. The plaintiff's negligence, if less than the amount attributable to the defendant or defendants, only serves to diminish recovery by the proportion of negligence attributable to the plaintiff...Thus, in a negligence action, the trier of fact must focus on the conduct of both the defendant and the plaintiff in determining the extent of each party's responsibility for the plaintiff's injuries. The plaintiff's conduct is not viewed as the sole proximate cause of the injury and does not bar recovery completely unless the plaintiff is more than fifty percent responsible for his or her own injuries.

Defined most simply, contributory negligence in products liability cases consists of the plaintiff's failure to discover the product's defect or to guard against the possibility that such a danger exists...Essentially, we require the plaintiff to act reasonably with respect to the product he or she is using. The plaintiff's contributory negligence is measured objectively.

In warranty, as in negligence, a plaintiff's conduct may bar recovery from a liable defendant. "The absolute bar to the user for breach of his duty balances the strict liability placed on the seller. Other than this instance, the parties are not presumed to be equally responsible for injuries caused by defective products, and the principles of contributory or comparative negligence have no part in the strict liability scheme."...Because warranty liability focuses on whether the product was defective and unreasonably dangerous, and not on the conduct of the user or the seller, "the only duty imposed on the user is to act reasonably with respect to a product which he knows to be defective and dangerous. When a user unreasonably proceeds to use a product which he knows to be defective and dangerous, he violates that duty and relinquishes the protection of the law. It is only then that it is appropriate to account for his conduct in determining liability. Since he has voluntarily relinquished the law's protection, it is further appropriate that he is barred from recovery."...The plaintiff's conduct implies consent to the risk and thus is viewed as the sole proximate cause of the injury...

Applying the unreasonable use doctrine to actions sounding in negligence is foreclosed by the Commonwealth's comparative negligence statute. That statute provides that a plaintiff's recovery shall not be barred by his or her contributory negligence unless the plaintiff's negligence is greater than the amount of negligence attributable to the parties against whom recovery is sought...The statute clearly defines the amount of contributory negligence that will bar the plaintiff's recovery. The defendant's suggestion that proof of unreasonable use in warranty should bar completely the plaintiff's recovery in negligence would, in effect, ordain that the plaintiff's unreasonable use of a product is, as a matter of law, negligence greater than that of the defendant's, and the sole proximate cause of the injury. That determination is, however, for the finder of fact to make on a case-by-case basis, and is not properly decided by the courts as a rule of law. In a negligence action, it is the function of the triers of fact to determine the percentage of fault attributable to the plaintiff, and the triers of fact are entitled to make that determination based on their perception of the relative fault of the parties. A jury may "...find that the plaintiff was barred because of his unreasonable action. That such unreasonable conduct on the part of the plaintiff may in this case also have been found by the jury to be contributory negligence...does not eradicate the distinction in the defenses to the two counts. Under the negligence count, the plaintiff is not barred unless his negligence is greater than the negligence of the persons against whom recovery is sought."...

Conclusion: We conclude that the jury's findings that Colter unreasonably proceeded to use the twin screw sand classifier after becoming aware of its defective condition does not bar recovery on his negligence claim as a matter of law. Nevertheless, we believe that application of some type of apportionment principles to warranty cases may be fairer than the current system, and may make results in negligence and warranty counts in the same case more consistent with each other. "[G]iven the wide variety of possible solutions,"..., and the serious policy considerations involved, the Legislature is the appropriate forum to select from among the competing proposals...

Assumption of the Risk

Assumption of the risk is a theory which recognizes that individuals sometimes knowingly do things which pose a threat to their safety. The rule is as follows: when a plaintiff knowingly confronts harm from a risk created by the defendant, he or she is held to have assumed that risk and therefore is barred from recovering for the defendant's negligence. While this is similar to the theory of comparative negligence, there is an important distinction between the two theories. Under a comparative negligence theory, the plaintiff acted negligently in regard to his or her own safety; that is, the plaintiff failed to act like a reasonable and prudent person. The theory of assumption of the risk imposes a more stringent criteria for its application. It is not enough that the plaintiff acted unreasonably, the plaintiff must have *knowingly* assumed the risk. It is certainly possible to act unreasonably without truly understanding (knowing) the consequences of one's actions. There are three elements which must be proven by the defendant to establish the defense of assumption of the risk: 1) the plaintiff had actual knowledge of the facts or circumstances creating the risk; 2) the plaintiff understood that these circumstances created a risk; and 3) the plaintiff had the opportunity to either confront or avoid the risk, and the plaintiff voluntarily chose to confront it.

The distinction between elements one and two is sometimes difficult to imagine; so for the sake of clarity, consider the following
admittedly simplistic, example. A two-year-old child may know
fire is hot because he or she has been told that is the case; but that
two-year-old child may not understand that because fire is hot, he
or she will get burned by touching it.

State-of-the-Art Defense

The state-of-the-art defense is sometimes raised by defendants
in product liability cases. Essentially, this defense asserts that given
the level of scientific and technical knowledge available at the
time the product was created, there were no feasible alternatives
which would have made the product safer. In short, the defendant
is saying: "I did the best I could; I acted as reasonably as possible
under the circumstances." Because the state-of-the-art defense
addresses the conduct of the defendant, it is not applicable to
strict liability claims which address the nature of the product.
Some States allow the state-of-the-art defense in negligence cases
which do focus on the reasonableness of the defendant's actions.

Beshada v. John-Manville Products Corporation is an example of a
case where the defendant attempted the state-of-the-art defense in
a strict liability lawsuit. This case is one of a family of cases against
this defendant involving exposure to asbestos allegedly resulting
in personal injuries and, in some cases, death. The plaintiffs claim
the defendant had an obligation to, among other things, warn
them of the dangers of exposure to asbestos. The defendant claims
that the state of the art was such that it had no knowledge of the
danger at the time of the exposures in question. In rejecting the
application of the state-of-the-art defense to a strict liability claim,
the court offers a detailed discussion of the nature of the defense
and its application. That portion of the case follows.

BESHADA v. JOHNS-MANVILLE PRODUCTS CORPORATION
Supreme Court of New Jersey
447 A.2d 539 (1982)

State-of-the-Art Defense: As it relates to warning cases, the state-of-the-art defense asserts that distributors of products can be held liable only for injuries resulting from dangers that were scientifically discoverable at the time the product was distributed. Defendants argue that the question of whether the product can be made safer must be limited to consideration of the available technology at the time the product was distributed. Liability would be absolute, defendants argue, if it could be imposed on the basis of a subsequently discovered means to make the product safer since technology will always be developing new ways to make products safer. Such a rule, they assert, would make manufacturers liable whenever their products cause harm, whether or not they are reasonably fit for their foreseeable purposes.

Defendants conceptualize the scientific unknowability of the dangerous propensities of a product as a technological barrier to making the product safer by providing warnings. Thus, a warning was not "possible" within the meaning of the *Freund* requirement that risk be reduced "to the greatest extent possible."

In urging this position, defendants must somehow distinguish the *Freund* holding that knowledge of the dangers of the product is imputed to defendants as a matter of law. A state-of-the-art defense would contravene that by requiring plaintiffs to prove at least that knowledge of the dangers was scientifically available at the time of manufacture.

Defendants argue that *Freund* did not specify precisely what knowledge is imputed to defendants. They construe *Freund* to impute only that degree of knowledge of the product's dangerousness that existed at the time of manufacture or distribution.

While we agree that *Freund* did not explicitly address this question, the principles laid down in *Freund* and our prior cases contradict a defendant's position. Essentially, state of the art is a negligence defense. It seeks to explain why defendants are not culpable for failing to provide a warning. They assert, in effect, that because they could not have known the product was dangerous, they acted reasonably in marketing it without a warning. But in strict liability cases, culpability is irrelevant. The product was unsafe. That it was unsafe because of the state of technology does not change the fact that it was unsafe. Strict liability focuses on the product, not the fault of the manufacturer. "If the conduct is unreasonably dangerous, then there is strict liability without reference to what excuse defendant might give for being unaware of the danger."...

When the defendants argue that it is unreasonable to impose a duty on them to warn of the unknowable, they misconstrue both the purpose and effect of strict liability. By imposing strict liability, we are not requiring defendants to have done something that is impossible. In this sense, the phrase "duty to warn" is misleading. It implies negligence concepts with their attendant focus on the reasonableness of defendant's behavior. However, a major concern of strict liability—ignored by defendant—is the conclusion that if a product was in fact defective, the distributor of the product should compensate its victims for the misfortune that it inflicted on them.

If we accepted the defendant's argument, we would create a distinction among fact situations that defies common sense. Under the defendant's reading of *Freund,* the defendant would be liable for failure to warn if the danger was knowable even if defendants were not negligent in failing to discover it. Defendants would suffer no liability, however, if the danger was undiscoverable. But, as Dean Keeton explains,

> if a defendant is to be held liable for a risk that is discoverable by some genius but beyond the defendant's capacity to do so, why should he not also be liable for a risk that was just as great but was not discoverable by anyone?...

We are buttressed in our conclusion that the state-of-the-art defense is inconsistent with *Freund* by [another recent decision] in which [the judge] applied New Jersey law to strike a defendant's state-of-the-art defense.

The most important inquiry, however, is whether imposition of liability for failure to warn of dangers which were undiscoverable at the time of manufacture will advance the goals and policies sought to be achieved by our strict liability rules. We believe that it will.

Risk Spreading—One of the most important arguments generally advanced for imposing strict liability is that the manufacturers and distributors of defective products can best allocate the costs of the injuries resulting from those products. The premise is that the price of a product should reflect all of its costs, including the cost of injuries caused by the product. This can best be accomplished by imposing liability on the manufacturer and distributors. Those persons can insure against liability and incorporate the cost of the insurance in the price of the product. In this way, the costs of the product will be borne by those who profit from it: the manufacturers and distributors who profit from its sale and the buyers who profit from its use. "It should be a cost of doing business that in the course of doing that business an unreasonable risk was created."...

Defendants argue that this policy is not forwarded by imposition of liability for unknowable hazards. Since such hazards by definition are not predicted, the price of the hazardous product will not be adjusted to reflect the costs of the injuries it will produce. Rather, defendants state, the cost "will be borne by the public at large and reflected in a general, across the board increase in premiums to compensate for unanticipated risks." There is some truth in this assertion, but it is not a bad result.

First, the same argument can be made as to hazards which are deemed scientifically knowable but of which the manufacturers are unaware. Yet it is well established under tort law that strict liability is imposed even for defects which were unknown to the manufacturer. It is precisely the imputation of knowledge to the defendant that distinguishes strict liability from negligence...Defendants advance no argument as to why risk spreading works better for unknown risks than for unknowable risks.

Second, spreading the costs of injuries among all those who produce, distribute, and purchase manufactured products is by far preferable to imposing it on the innocent victims who suffer illnesses and disability from defective products. This basic normative premise is at the center of our strict liability rules. It is unchanged by the state of scientific knowledge at the time of manufacture.

Finally, contrary to the defendant's assertion, this rule will not cause the price and production level of manufactured products to diverge from the so-called economically efficient level. Rather, the rule will force the price of any particular product to reflect the cost of insuring against the possibility that the product will turn out to be defective.

Accident Avoidance—In *Suter,* we stated:

Strict liability in a sense is but an attempt to minimize the costs of accidents and to consider who should bear those costs. [In one law review article the authors persuasively] suggest that the strict liability issue is to decide which party is the 'cheapest cost avoider' or who is in the best position to make the cost-benefit analysis between accident costs and accident avoidance costs and to act on that decision once it is made...Using this approach, it is obvious that the manufacturer rather than the factory employee is 'in the better position both to judge whether avoidance costs would exceed foreseeable accident costs and to act on that judgment.'...

Defendants urge that this argument has no force as to hazards which, by definition, were undiscoverable. Defendants have treated the level of technological knowledge at a given time as an independent variable not affected by the defendants' conduct. But this view ignores the important role of industry in product safety research. The "state of the art" at a given time is partly determined by how much industry invests in safety research. By imposing on manufacturers the costs of failure to discover hazards, we create an incentive for them to invest more actively in safety research.

Fact-Finding Process—The analysis thus far has assumed that it is possible to define what constitutes "undiscoverable" knowledge, and that it

will be reasonably possible to determine what knowledge was techno-
logically discoverable at a given time. In fact, both assumptions are highly questionable. The vast confusion that is virtually certain to arise from
any attempt to deal in a trial setting with the concept of scientific
knowability constitutes a strong reason for avoiding the concept alto-
gether by striking the state-of-the-art defense.

Scientific knowability, as we understand it, refers not to what in fact
was known at the time, but to what *could have been* known at the time.
In other words, even if no scientist had actually formed the belief that
asbestos was dangerous, the hazards would be deemed "knowable" if a
scientist could have formed that belief by applying research or performing tests that were available at the time. Proof of what could have been
known will inevitably be complicated, costly, confusing, and time consuming. Each side will have to produce experts in the history of science
and technology to speculate as to what knowledge was feasible in a
given year. We doubt that juries will be capable of even understanding
the concept of scientific knowability, much less be able to resolve such a
complex issue. Moreover, we should resist legal rules that will so greatly
add to the costs both sides incur in trying a case.

The concept of knowability is complicated further by the fact, noted
above, that the level of investment in safety research by manufacturers is
one determinant of the state of the art at any given time. Fairness suggests that manufacturers not be excused from liability because their prior
inadequate investment in safety rendered the hazards of their product
unknowable. Thus, a judgment will have to be made as to whether the
defendants' investment in safety research in the years preceding distribution of the product was adequate. If not, the experts in the history of
technology will have to testify as to what would have been knowable at
the time of distribution if manufacturers had spent the proper amount
on safety in prior years. To state the issue is to fully understand the great
difficulties it would engender in a courtroom.

In addition, discussion of state of the art could easily confuse juries
into believing that blameworthiness is at issue. Juries might mistakenly
translate the confused concept of state of the art into the simple one of

whether it was the defendants' fault that they did not know of the hazards of asbestos. But that would be negligence, not strict liability.

. . .

For the reasons expressed above, we conclude that the plaintiff's position is consistent without holding in *Freund* and prior cases, and will achieve the various policies underlying strict liability. The burden of illness from dangerous products such as asbestos should be placed upon those who profit from its production and, more generally, upon society at large, which reaps the benefits of the various products our economy manufactures. That burden should not be imposed exclusively on the innocent victim. Although victims must in any case suffer the pain involved, they should be spared the burdensome financial consequences of unfit products. At the same time, we believe this position will serve the salutary goals of increasing product safety research and simplifying tort trials.

Defendants have argued that it is unreasonable to impose a duty on them to warn of the unknowable. Failure to warn of a risk which one could not have known existed is not unreasonable conduct. But this argument is based on negligence principles. We are not saying what defendants should have done. That is negligence. We are saying that defendants' products were not reasonably safe because they did not have a warning. Without a warning, users of the product were unaware of its hazards and could not protect themselves from injury. We impose strict liability because it is unfair for the distributors of a defective product not to compensate its victims. As between those innocent victims and the distributors, it is the distributors—and the public which consumes their products—which should bear the unforeseen costs of the product.

The judgment of the trial court is reversed; the plaintiff's motion to strike the state-of-the-art defense is granted.

Proving a Case

Much of the mystery of law is found, not in substantive law, but in procedural law. As pointed out earlier, procedural law is the body of law which governs the mechanics of a lawsuit. The following will focus on the methods by which a lawsuit is commenced and proven. For the purposes of this discussion, only civil lawsuits will be considered, bearing in mind that the processes governing criminal lawsuits are different.

Commencement of a Lawsuit

A lawsuit is started when the plaintiff's attorney files a complaint with the appropriate court. A typical complaint (among other things) states who is being sued, the legal theory or theories on which liability is alleged, the factual basis of the alleged wrongdoing, the nature of the damages alleged, and the amount of money sought to compensate the plaintiff for his or her injuries. It is important to note that a complaint may, as a number of the case examples cited earlier did, allege liability on more than one legal theory. For example, in a product liability action, a plaintiff may sue for breach of warranty and negligence. Conventional legal wisdom says it does not matter which hook a judge hangs his or her hat on, as long as it is hung. Consequently, a plaintiff's attorney will consider all possibilities in drafting a complaint in an effort to give a judge every opportunity to agree with the plaintiff's position.

After the complaint is filed and the defendant has been notified of the lawsuit, the defendant is given a period of time to file an answer. That is, the defendant must then respond to each allegation in the complaint. To the extent a defendant agrees or disagrees with particular allegations, the exact nature of the litigation begins to take form. This is because the only issues to be addressed in a trial are the ones over which the plaintiff and defendant disagree. If they agree, at the time of the trial, they stipulate to those facts. In fact, a defendant may admit to having done everything alleged in the complaint, but continue to claim no liability on the grounds that what he or she did is not against the law. For example, psychiatrists have a legal obligation to keep confidential all communications from patients unless a patient has given permission to publicly disclose such information. What if a psychiatrist is writing a textbook of case studies and uses a patient's history without the patient's consent, but omits the patient's name? Is this a breach of confidentiality? In other words, in cases such as this, the dispute is not over issues of fact, but over an issue of law. The purpose of stipulations is to save the time and expense of establishing facts which are not in dispute.

Discovery Phase

After the answer to the complaint has been filed, the lawsuit moves into the discovery phase. Discovery is the point at which each side is allowed to see the opponent's evidence. It is only at the discovery phase that each side has the legal right to compel the opponent to disclose their evidence. Consequently, it is not until discovery that the attorneys for the parties can see objectively (as opposed to through the eyes of their clients) whether a client is lying, and beyond that, the relative strength of their client's case. This is extremely helpful in determining whether the case should go to trial, be dropped, or settled. In addition, it can be very helpful in arriving at a more concrete valuation of the damages alleged. One criticism frequently leveled at the legal profession is that too many frivolous cases are brought. While it is certainly not true in all cases, in many, a case is known by the attorney to be frivolous *only after* discovery. As pointed out earlier, until the discovery phase of litigation, an attorney has no right or mechanism by which to require the opponent to divulge his or her evidence. Consequently, a case which started out to appear to be reasonably solid turns out to be unsubstantiated or weak as the evidence is disclosed in the discovery process.

There are three major discovery techniques utilized in most litigation: *interrogatories, requests for the production of documents,* and *depositions.* Interrogatories are written questions presented by one party to the other, including witnesses. The party receiving the interrogatories must respond truthfully. While the law requires the responding party to answer truthfully, standard practice is to answer the questions as narrowly as possible. That is, the strategy is to tell the truth, but to divulge as little of it as possible. In addition to providing evidence on which to assist the opposing party to evaluate the overall case, the answers to interrogatories may be used in court for various purposes. Generally, the answers to interrogatories cannot be used in lieu of live testimony (unless a witness had died in the meantime), but the answers can be used, for example, to challenge the credibility of a witness who gives one answer in the interrogatories and another during the trial.

Requests for the production of documents are used to find out what kind of written documentation exists which may be relevant to the case. For example, in product liability litigation, the plaintiff will want to see all paperwork relative to the design, production, and testing of the product. In addition, all records of such things as customer complaints and repairs will be sought. The party making such requests is entitled to inspect, copy, and photograph the documents. A party who believes he or she is being asked to produce documents which are not legally subject to discovery can ask a judge to so rule. Otherwise, the documents must be provided to the opponent.

Depositions involve a party or witness being deposed (questioned) by the opposing attorney in a face-to-face forum. Typically, the party seeking the deposition holds it in his or her office. Present are the attorneys for both sides, and a stenographer who records everything said (except when the attorneys agree to go off the record). Depositions serve a number of purposes. First, like all other discovery techniques, the opposing party's evidence is exposed. Second, the opposing attorney gets an idea of how good a witness this individual will be in trial. Because this is one of the things the attorney is attempting to assess, some attorneys will deliberately harass and badger witnesses in depositions just to see if it works. If a witness can be rattled and thrown off track in the deposition, the attorney is likely to attempt the same thing in the trial. Third, like the answers to interrogatories, the responses to questions in depositions can be used to challenge a witness during the trial if the witness gives different answers to the same question.

A word on surprise witnesses—Perry Mason notwithstanding, such television and movie ploys as the surprise witness are not the lifeblood of the legal profession. As a matter of fact, the surprise witness is virtually impossible under the rules of procedure in Federal courts and most State courts. This is because one of the requests routinely allowed in discovery is a list of the opponent's prospective witnesses, including a summary of the substance of their expected testimony. It makes for great drama, but is not consistent with most notions of a fair hearing.

Another dramatic courtroom tactic can be found in virtually every episode of "L.A. Law"—the eloquent closing argument complete with the latest statistics on the topic of the day. In closing arguments, attorneys are restricted to commenting *only* on matters already introduced into evidence. If it did not come out of the mouth of a witness, it cannot be addressed, no matter now compelling. Lawyers who run afoul of this limitation run the risk of a mistrial for their client.

The Trial

The trial starts with the opening statements of each attorney. This is followed by the plaintiff's presentation of his or her side of the case. When the plaintiff has called all of his or her witnesses, the defense presents its side of the case. During the presentation of evidence by the witnesses, it is common for the opposing attorney to object either to the substance or form of the question, or the qualifications of the witness, or to the form of an answer given by a witness. Deciding what to object to and how frequently involves an assessment of two things: the technical rules of law (e.g., for someone to offer a medical opinion, one must be trained as a physician) and the appearance created in the minds of the jurors. For example, at some points, an attorney will not object to an objectionable line of questioning because no damage is being done, and the attorney does not want to create the appearance that there is anything to hide. Similarly, an attorney does not want to object so much that the jury gets annoyed or distracted by the interruptions. In the final analysis, there are two reasons for raising objections. The first is simply that a rule of procedure or evidence is being violated. Second, it is during the trial that the record is established for any appeal which may follow. To protect a party's right of appeal, the record must be "perfected." For example, in most cases the losing party cannot appeal claiming a piece of evidence was improperly admitted in the first trial *unless* an objection was raised during the first trial.

Jury Instructions

At the conclusion of a jury trial, the judge instructs the jury as to the law which is applicable to the case. Given the power of words generally, and a lawyer's ability to twist words specifically (it is part of the training), the precise wording of the instructions is important. Consequently, the lawyers for each side of the case are entitled to submit proposed instructions to the judge. The judge then evaluates the instructions and decides which instructions to use. The final instructions selected will be any combination of the instructions proposed by the plaintiff's attorney, the defendant's attorney, and those developed by the judge himself or herself. The following provides a sample of proposed instructions, from a defendant's perspective, for a product liability lawsuit involving the following issues: negligence, failure to warn, contributory negligence, and a breach of warranty. These instructions are based on Massachusetts law. Consequently, instructions for cases in the courts of other States will vary.

For ease of reading, headings have been inserted to highlight the general topics of the instructions. You will notice that some of the instructions are repetitive. For example, instructions 15 and 16 deal with the circumstances under which a warning is legally required. If the judge concludes such an instruction is appropriate, there are two to choose from. From the perspective of the defendant's attorney, offering two alternatives to the judge increases the probability that some instruction will be given on this issue. You will also notice that there are innumerable places in the instructions where the defendant's name is to be inserted. This is intended to personalize the defendant to the jury. The defense attorney wants the jury to see the defendant in concrete terms, not as an impersonal individual or organization. Yes, the defendant's attorney is attempting to garner exactly what that same attorney's proposed instructions (2 and 3) warn the jurors against—sympathy for one of the parties to the lawsuit.

DEFENDANT'S REQUESTS FOR JURY INSTRUCTIONS[16]

Now comes the defendant, and respectfully requests this Honorable Court to instruct the jury as follows.

Evidence and Facts

1. You are not to be concerned with the statements made by counsel throughout the trial. These are not evidence unless adopted by a witness on direct or cross examination. You are not to be concerned with the objections made by counsel throughout the course of the trial during the examination of witnesses, the reading of deposition transcripts, or the introduction of documents. Counsel is obligated to make these objections and you are not to consider them in rendering your verdict. You are also to disregard any evidence which the judge has ordered to be stricken from the record.

2. You cannot be governed by sympathy or prejudice or any motive whatsoever, except a fair and impartial consideration of the evidence, and you must not allow any sympathy you may have for any party to influence you in any degree

---

[16]*Source:* Products Liability Basics, Boston, MA: Massachusetts Continuing Legal Education, Inc., 1990.

whatever, in deciding whether the plaintiffs have sustained their burden or proof, or in assessing damages.

3. The corporate defendant in this case is entitled to the same fair and unprejudiced treatment by a jury as an individual would be under like circumstances, and the jury should decide the case between the individuals.

4. The jury, in finding the cause of the plaintiff's injury, can only reach conclusions on facts which have been proven, and by rational inferences drawn from those proven facts.

Burden of Proof

5. The burden of proof is on the plaintiff to prove each and every essential element of his/her claim by a preponderance of all the credible evidence. If the evidence should fail to establish any one of the essential elements of the plaintiff's claims, or if the evidence is equally balanced as to any of the essential elements of the plaintiff's claims, then you must find for the defendant.

6. If on all the credible evidence you find that it is just as reasonable to believe that the cause of the plaintiff's alleged injury is one for which no liability would attach to [defendant's name] as one for which [defendant's name] is liable, the plaintiff has failed to sustain his/her burden of proof and you must find for the defendants.

Negligence Claim

7. The mere happening of an injury, no matter how serious, is not evidence of negligence or breach of warranty on the part of the defendant.

8. In order to recover for negligence against [defendant's name], the plaintiff must prove by a preponderance of the evidence three essential elements: (a) that the defendant owed a duty to the plaintiff under all the circumstances; (b) that the

defendant breached that duty; and (c) that the breach of that duty caused the injury sustained by the plaintiff.

9. In order for the plaintiff to recover, he/she must prove that the injury came from an act of negligence for which [defendant's name] is responsible. If you find that the accident resulted from the act or omission of another person or entity for which [defendant's name] is not responsible, then you must find for the defendant.

10. The plaintiff has the burden of proving by a preponderance of all the credible evidence not only that [defendant's name] was negligent, but that the plaintiff was injured as a direct and proximate result of this negligence.

11. You must find that the defendant, [defendant's name], is not liable if you find that any negligence of the defendant was superseded by the intervening negligence of a third person. By superseding cause I mean the action of someone other than [defendant's name] that becomes the real cause of the plaintiff's damages and brings the damages about regardless of any negligence on the part of [defendant's name].

Failure to Warn

12. In order for the plaintiff to recover on a theory of negligent failure by [defendant's name] to warn of a dangerous condition, the plaintiff must show that a warning would have reduced the likelihood of injury. Negligent failure to warn is not the proximate cause of an injury when a warning would not have eliminated the possibility of injuries, or was not necessary due to the plaintiff's experience and expertise, and therefore the plaintiff cannot recover.

13. In order for the plaintiff to recover on a theory of negligent failure by [defendant's name] to warn of a dangerous condition, the plaintiff must show that a warning would reduce the likelihood of injury. Negligent failure to warn is not the

proximate cause of an injury when a warning would not eliminate the possibility of injuries. A user of a product is obliged to exercise due care in the use of the product. Responsible and diligent efforts by the user contribute to the prevention of accidents.

14. The duty to warn extends only to concealed, nonobvious dangers. When the danger is obvious, a warning would be superfluous. There is no duty to warn of such dangers.

15. There must be a reason or belief that a warning is needed.

16. In the law of torts, there is, in general, no duty to warn unless the person on whom the duty rests has some reason to suppose that a warning is needed.

17. The designer of a product has no duty to warn of an obvious danger connected with the use of the product or to warn someone who already knows of the danger.

Plaintiff's Contributory Negligence

18. The law requires that a plaintiff act as a reasonable person would under the circumstances to avoid a foreseeable risk of harm. If you find that the plaintiff did not exercise reasonable care for his/her own safety, you must also find that he/she was negligent.

19. As to what constitutes contributory negligence, there is no substantial difference between "want or lack of due care" and "contributory negligence." Both terms refer to the kind and degree of care for one's own safety that an ordinary reasonable person would exercise under the same circumstances. Care imports attention, heedfulness, and caution.

20. "Care imports attention, heedfulness, caution; and to use or take any degree of care there must be some vigilance,

some exercise of the faculties to preserve what it is desirable to save, or to avoid the danger or avert the peril to which a person may be exposed."

Speculation Versus Proof

21. The plaintiff may not recover if the precise cause of the injuries is not known. If guesswork or speculation are necessary to determine the cause of the injuries, you must find that the defendant did not breach any warranty.

22. An act or omission on the part of [defendant's name] will not provide grounds for relief unless the plaintiff shows that the act or omission was a substantial cause in bringing about the plaintiff's injuries.

23. The plaintiff has failed to maintain the burden of proof if, on all of the credible evidence, the question of the defendant's negligence or breach of warranty is left to conjecture, surmise, or speculation.

24. It is not enough for the plaintiff to prove that the accident might have—or could have—resulted from the negligence or breach of warranty of [defendant's name]. The plaintiff must show that it is more likely than not that it did. If you find that the accident was not caused by negligence or breach of warranty on the part of [defendant's name], then you must return a verdict in the defendant's favor.

25. The plaintiffs here are bound to introduce enough credible evidence to remove the cause of the injury from the realm of speculation. In this case, mere speculation as to the cause of the injury is not sufficient to allow you to render a verdict against [defendant's name].

Intervening Causes

26. If you find that the conduct of someone other than

[defendant's name] was the sole proximate cause of the plaintiff's accident, then you must return a verdict for [defendant's name]. This conduct may be the negligence of another defendant and/or the negligence of the plaintiff.

27. If you find that the manner in which the plaintiff conducted his or her duties that day probably would have resulted in the accident regardless of how the [allegedly offending product] was designed, manufactured, or installed, you must find for the defendant.

28. If the plaintiff's accident was caused solely by his or her own negligence, and not to any degree by any negligence of any defendant, then he or she is not entitled to recover damages from any defendant.

29. If you find that the plaintiff believed the [allegedly offending product] was dangerous and continued to use it, or that he or she used it in an unreasonable manner and such use was the sole cause of his or her injuries, [plaintiff's name] is not entitled to recover damages from any defendant even if any defendant or any third person was negligent.

Foreseeability of Risk

30. Any legal duty owned by the defendant, [defendant's name], existed only to the extent that he or she could reasonably foresee the risk of injury to such a person as the plaintiff.

31. Unless the plaintiff proves by a fair preponderance of the evidence that the accident which resulted in the injury to the plaintiff reasonably was foreseeable by the defendant, you must find for [defendant's name].

Negligent Infliction of Emotional Distress

32. To recover for emotional distress caused by a negligent act, a plaintiff must prove that the defendant was (a) negligent;

(b) that emotional distress followed the negligent act closely in time; (c) that the negligent act caused the emotional distress; (d) that physical harm manifested by objective symptomatology resulted from the injury; and (e) that a reasonable person would have suffered emotional distress under the circumstances of the case.

Breach of Warranty

33. The defendant may not be found liable for breach of warranty unless you determine all the following facts: (a) that the product was unreasonably dangerous; (b) that the defendant knew of the risks presented by its product; and (c) that the defendant failed to issue adequate warnings.

34. [Defendant's name] was not bound to foresee and guard against events which were apparently impossible or highly improbable. Warranty liability is not absolute liability. A manufacturer must design only against the reasonably foreseeable risks attending the product's use. The manufacturer is not bound to design an excellent or foolproof product. A manufacturer is only required to use reasonable care in the design of the product, taking into account the state of the art. A manufacturer is not liable if the product's design did not cause the plaintiff's injuries.

35. A designer is not required to design the safest possible product or to design against all possible risks and imaginable dangers, however remote.

36. The issue in a design negligence case is not whether a safer alternative design was available but whether the manufacturer exercised reasonable care to design out avoidable dangers.

37. The law requires a person who designs a product to use the knowledge and skill of a reasonable person in the same circumstances.

Impact of Expert Witness Testimony

38. "Experts can be found to testify to anything." Therefore, there is no obligation for you to believe an expert witness merely because he or she is an expert witness. You are free to reject his or her testimony in whole or in part if you are not satisfied that it is based on the facts of the case as you find them to be, if you find that he or she does not have a sufficient basis on which to support his or her opinion, if you find that he or she has not had a sufficient opportunity to observe that which he or she purports to have observed, or if you find that his or her opinion is motivated by his or her interest in the case.

39. A verdict may not be based on conjecture or surmise; and expert opinion is not beneficial if it is demonstrated that it rests on speculation.

40. A guess or conjecture by an expert witness has no evidential value.

41. Where it is demonstrated during the testimony of an expert that his or her opinion rests wholly on reasons which are legally incompetent, there is no right to have his or her opinion considered as evidence.

Factors Affecting Damage Award

42. In assessing damages for any future losses of the plaintiff because of the loss of the plaintiff's income, you should reduce these damages by the amount of income taxes on the plaintiff's estimated future earnings.

43. In assessing damages for any future losses of the plaintiff, you should not consider possible future inflationary trends.

44. In assessing damages for any future losses of the plaintiff, the law requires you to reduce these future damages to their "present value" to allow for the interest that will be earned in the future on any verdict rendered today. You must

consider the interest that will be earned in the future, and reduce any verdict accordingly, so that the plaintiff will not recover more than the just compensation you determine.

45. The clerk will, if there is an award of money, add interest onto this award at the statutory rate of interest applicable to this case. The purpose of interest is to compensate the plaintiff for the loss of the use of that money should he or she be entitled to any money.

46. The statutory rate of interest applicable to this case is 12% per annum.

47. An award by you of monies is not taxable by the State or Federal government. Consequently, you are not to take into consideration income taxes.

This last group of instructions deals with the issue of computing damages in the event the jury finds against the defendant. It suggests guidance relative to the tax consequences of judgments, the impact of inflation, and applicable interest rates. Offering instructions on these issues is risky. While many jurors will understand these issues in a general sense, they may not understand how to take them into account in their assessment of damages (and this assumes they have access to a calculator, which may or may not be true). Consequently, it may be wiser not to muddy the waters, and simply permit their collective wisdom and common sense to dictate reason.

Appeals

The losing party to a lawsuit may have grounds for appealing to the next higher court. However, there are serious limitations on the right of appeal. First, as noted earlier, most appeals require an appropriate objection to have been raised at the original trial. No objection—no appeal. (One might have a case of malpractice against the erring attorney, however.) Second, with extremely limited exceptions, appeals are limited to issues of law only (as opposed to issues of fact). What this means is that a party cannot appeal a case simply because the jury decided to believe the other party's version of the story—even if the losing party was telling the truth and the winning party lied. While this might appear to be a harsh rule, the alternative must be considered. If anyone could appeal anything, there would literally be no end to litigation. Some limitations have to be placed on the process. Judgments concerning the credibility of witnesses are issues of fact. Issues of law, in contrast, involve such things as whether the rules of evidence were properly applied, the jury instructions were correctly stated, and the correct rule of substantive law was applied.

Evidentiary Issues in Product Liability Cases

Evidence is what is used to prove a case. The preceding chapter provided a general overview of the mechanical process involved in proving a case. This chapter will focus on more technical aspects of the types of evidentiary issues which frequently arise in product liability litigation. There are two purposes in this. The first is to provide some insight into the types of circumstances which call for seeking legal counsel. The second is to highlight the significance of having done so should litigation result. It must be emphasized that the purpose of early involvement by an attorney *is not* to suggest that an attorney's advice should or must be followed over the professional judgment of an engineer in regard to engineering matters. The point is that engineering (and other professional) judgments can have legal consequences. The *best professional judgment* is made by an informed person who is aware of both the technical nuances *and* legal risks associated with various courses of action. With this in mind, the following will be considered: the nature of direct and circumstantial evidence, corporate record keeping policies, and the attorney–client privilege.

Direct and Circumstantial Evidence

There are essentially two types of evidence which may be used in any type of lawsuit: direct evidence and circumstantial evidence. Direct evidence is exactly what the name implies; it speaks directly to the matter in question without requiring any reading between the lines. In a personal injury lawsuit, it may take the form of eye witness testimony from those who saw the accident. In a breach of contract action, it would include such things as the original, signed contracts. This is not to suggest that direct evidence is infallible. An eye witness may have been hampered by poor lighting or a partially obstructed view. An original, signed contract can be incomplete if there were subsequent modifications.

Circumstantial evidence is different in that it does require reading between the lines; that is, it requires an inference to be drawn. For example, in a homicide case, the fact that a witness heard a noise which *sounded like* a gunshot is circumstantial evidence. In the absence of the witness having contemporaneously seen the defendant pull the trigger, at least two inferences must be drawn from this testimony before a conclusion can be drawn that the defendant fired a gun. First, an inference must be made that the noise was, in fact, a gunshot as opposed to something like a car backfiring. Second, an inference must be drawn that the defendant pulled the trigger. With a credible witness, the first inference may be made without a great deal of difficulty. However, the second inference is difficult without additional corroborating evidence linking the defendant to the gunshot. Note that even if both inferences are reasonably made, all that has been established is that the defendant discharged the gun. If it was done in self-defense, there is no homicide.

While both direct evidence and circumstantial evidence are valid types of evidence, direct evidence is stronger. That is, it is more persuasive, and it is easier to convince a judge or jury with direct evidence. Nevertheless, entire cases can be and have been successfully tried with circumstantial evidence only.

Corporate Record Keeping

Internal company documents concerning the product in question are critical to the defense in product liability litigation. The first step in any product liability defense is to gather as much information as possible. The types of information sought fall into two general categories. One category comprises all documents concerning the development of the product, such as the design, manufacture, testing, inspection, and redesign (if any) of the product. The second category of records relates to what happened after the product was sold to consumers. It includes such things as repair records, customer complaints, accident reports, and recall programs. All of these records should be maintained through an appropriate records retention policy. If a company does not have such a formal policy, one should be developed in consultation with an attorney experienced in product liability litigation.

The picture an attorney hopes to paint with these documents is a simple one. The product was designed, manufactured, tested, inspected, and sold following proper procedures, safety standards, and laws. In addition, consumer complaints and problems were addressed promptly and appropriately.

In some cases, a company's internal documents paint the wrong picture, or, at a minimum, are subject to varying interpretations. Consequently, it may be tempting to circumvent this problem by destroying or "losing" the records in question. This approach is dangerous and usually illegal.

The law *is* perfectly clear in stating that it is illegal to dispose of documents relevant to litigation. In fact, this prohibition extends beyond those situations where a lawsuit has been formally filed. If a defendant knows a lawsuit will be filed, or that it is possible in the future, all relevant documents must be retained (even if the company's record retention policy would otherwise call for their disposal).

The legal consequences of failing to retain such records can be severe. One possible outcome is that the judge will instruct the jury that it may infer the missing or destroyed documents contained evidence damaging to the defendant. In an extreme case, where the judge concludes the destruction of documents was done in "bad faith," the judge can enter a default judgment against the defendant on the basis of the missing documents. A third possible consequence is that the plaintiff will file another lawsuit against the defendant for "spoilation of evidence." In States which permit this claim, it serves as a civil counterpart to the criminal rule against obstructing justice. A defendant who illegally destroys evidence may be required to pay civil damages for that misconduct.

There is one readily available course of action which may be taken regarding potentially damaging internal documents (others will be discussed later). It is simply that of consulting with legal counsel at the time the information first comes to light. Do not wait for the lawsuit or threat thereof years down the road. There may be a course of action or response which can minimize the possibility of the documents being problematic later. For example, it is discovered that an employee "fudged" test results out of fear of an overbearing superior. Legal counsel can offer advice about how to create an appropriate paper trail of the corrective measures taken regarding new tests and their accurate documentation.

Attorney–Client Privilege

The attorney–client privilege protects all confidential communications between an attorney and client for the purpose of giving or obtaining legal advice. The privilege applies to both conversations and written communications. Further, it applies even though a lawsuit has not been filed. Because the privilege applies even though a lawsuit has not been filed, it can be particularly useful in a preventative sense. For example, an incident occurs which requires an in-house investigation. If an attorney is *not* used in this investigation, a plaintiff is likely to be given access to the results if a lawsuit is filed later. However, if an attorney is appropriately involved in the investigation, it is possible to claim the attorney–client privilege and thereby prevent the disclosure of the results of the investigation; that is, the information from the investigation *cannot* become part of the evidence used in any subsequent lawsuit.

One of the difficulties in applying the attorney–client privilege doctrine in the context of a corporation is that of identifying the client. A corporate defendant is very different from a criminal defendant, for example. In many if not most cases, an attorney who represents a corporation cannot point to a single individual who is the "client." But the privilege applies only to communications between an attorney and a *client*. The general rule in the corporate context is that the *client* is any corporate employee who communicates with an attorney at the direction of management in regard to actual or proposed conduct which falls within the scope of his or her employment. This rule underscores the need for company policies which instruct employees to seek specific legal advice concerning various courses of action when situations arise which are likely to have legal consequences. It further underscores the need of management-level personnel to be sensitive to this in those "out-of-the-normal-course-of-things" situations which arise in any business.

A second difficulty in applying the attorney–client privilege in the corporate context is that of maintaining confidentiality. By the very nature of the corporate structure, many situations will arise in which the communications occur between an attorney and group of corporate employees. To maintain the claim that the communications are privileged, it must be established that they are, in fact, confidential in nature (as opposed to communications which are meant for general circulation to all employees, for example). There are a number of ways to minimize this problem. First, legally sensitive information and documents should be communicated to employees on a "need-to-know" basis only. Second, the documents should be secured with access limited again to those who have a "need to know." Third, sensitive documents should be labelled with an appropriate reminder such as "CONFIDENTIAL" or "ATTORNEY–CLIENT PRIVILEGE." Fourth, the number of copies which are circulated should be kept to a minimum, and recipients should be reminded of their sensitivity, that they are not to be copied, and that they are to be returned when no longer needed.

It goes without saying that it is impossible to develop a strategy which renders any business immune from the possibility of a lawsuit. Nevertheless, careful planning in the development and implementation of in-house policies is critical to minimizing the probability of such a claim and to minimizing the damage if it cannot be avoided.

Product Liability—Beyond the Law: An Essay

As important as the law is, it is nonetheless minimalist in nature. That is, it establishes the minimally acceptable standards of conduct within society. Anyone whose conduct falls below those standards runs the risk of being sanctioned by the authority of the government through the mechanisms of the legal system. If the law operates at the minimal level, what operates beyond? In a word—ethics.

Both in business and in the professions, ethics became one of the watchwords of the 1980's. As we move into the 1990's, there are no signs of its waning. It is not that ethics is new—that no one has heard of it before. What appears to be happening is that the collective American society is struggling in a search to respond adequately to a number of scandals and excesses which have been front page fodder over the past two decades. How did it come to be that a President of the United States engaged in the Watergate break-in? Did Ronald Reagan (and others) lie to Congress and the American people about the Iran-Contra Affair? Were Ronald Reagan's memory lapses credible? If the answer is yes, did we do a disservice to ourselves in allowing him to be President? Was Ronald Reagan, and perhaps even George Bush, involved in a delay of the release of hostages in an effort to embarrass or upstage Jimmy Carter and the Democratic Party? Are Americans expected to really believe that Gerald Ford's pardon of Nixon three weeks after being sworn into office was a coincidence? What level of arrogance did Gary Hart possess in his challenge to the press? Is the Kennedy citadel wavering in the wake of the latest apparent scandal involving Willie Smith? And what about the masters of insider trading and leveraged buyouts? How many millions of dollars does one person need to live comfortably, and at what expense to everyone else? Who is responsible for all the bank failures? Should Exxon get a tax deduction for the money it pays to settle the lawsuits following the Alaskan oil spill? Did Pete Rose bet on baseball? Should he be allowed into the Hall of Fame?

All of these events, if assumed true (and I do not claim to know if they all are or not), raise the same questions. Was it the right thing to do? And if the answer is no, how did these people come to do wrong? Were they driven by a thirst for money, power, status?

At the risk of oversimplification, to the extent any of the foregoing examples qualify as wrongdoing, I submit they result from short-term and self-centered thinking. Individuals do not factor in the long-range impact. They disregard or discount the impact of their conduct on others. In some cases, the impact on others is direct and concrete harm. For example, if Willie Smith did rape the woman in Florida, he physically and emotionally hurt her. In other cases, the harm is less direct, and perhaps more insidious. Richard Nixon hurt the American system of democratic self-governance. On one level, it is true that the system worked—he was removed from office without a coup or some other dramatic turn of events which we are accustomed to witnessing in other countries with less stable governments. This is grounds to give one renewed faith in the American way. But this renewed faith is a faint glimmer compared to the damage he wreaked in betraying the American people. On a level to which I can find no relevant comparison, his engaging in and subsequent handling of Watergate left generations of American people with a depth of cynicism and distrust previously unknown in American history. It is not that there are no good, honest politicians today. It is not that we did not have crooked politicians before. The legacy of Nixon's betrayal of the American people is that we no longer have a basis for judging who is good and honest, and who is not. So we err on the side of being skeptical, at best, to being completely distrustful of all of them, at worst. We do not dare trust anyone because we might be wrong. We have been wrong too many times before.

Now, what does all this have to do with engineers plying their profession? All of us are confronted with choices in our lives which have the potential for doing harm to others. Fortunately, most of us can go about making these decisions without the public scrutiny to which politicians, professional athletes, corporate giants, and other celebrities are subjected. This distinction, however, does not make our decisions less significant. Just as they have the capacity to do harm to others, so do we. And I submit we are more likely to do that if we engage in short-term self-centered thinking. This is not to suggest that taking oneself into account is inherently wrong. The crux of the matter is in how one takes oneself into account—and it rarely should be done completely at the expense of anyone or everyone else. It is difficult to imagine many of the previously cited events occurring if two simple principles were honored. First, do unto others as you would have them do unto you. Second, when in doubt, do the right thing.

I am still somewhat afield from the specific concerns of engineers and product liability issues. So, consider this. It is axiomatic to observe that engineers are different from most other service professionals. Doctors, lawyers, and accountants provide services to individual clients. Any malpractice or ethical lapses which occur are fairly readily traceable to a particular practitioner. Furthermore, such lapses on the part of such professionals tend to negatively impact on the individual client only. This is not the case with engineers.

In contrast, engineers tend to work either in teams or on pieces of projects. They are involved in the design and production of products and processes. The results of these group efforts impact on individuals *and on society*. The impact of such things as nuclear power plants and pollution control systems affect society today and for generations to come. Furthermore, while many people go through life without engaging the services of an accountant or a lawyer, and some without seeing a doctor, it is virtually impossible in American society to avoid the products and processes created by the engineer. One would have to live in a home without the modern conveniences of plumbing, electricity, appliances, and tools of virtually any kind. In addition, one would have to stay there. Any form of transportation short of walking or horseback (or the like) utilizes the products of engineers' efforts—bicycles, cars, trucks, buses, subways, trains, or planes. Consequently, engineers are *not* unlike politicians, professional athletes, the masters of business, and other celebrities. While they lack the spotlight, engineers are like the others in that their "misdeeds" have the potential for broadly impacting on society at large. Consider for a moment the explosion of the *Challenger*, the B.F. Goodrich brake scandal, the problems with the design and development of the Bay Area Rapid Transit System.

Before exploring how engineers might approach evaluating the ethical quality of their conduct, I would like to say a few words about why people sometimes do the wrong thing. First, it is important to set aside those situations which, with hindsight, prove to be bad judgments, but which involved no ill will or unprofessional conduct. Regardless of the profession, people are sometimes compelled to make decisions with less time and/or information than is ideal or even desirable. Hindsight may show there was a better choice—this does not mean the original judgment was wrong or unethical. My concern here is with judgments which are unethical because there was malice or reckless disregard for the consequences of the course of conduct; or where the stakes were of a magnitude that demanded further inquiry even though that was not convenient, expedient, or popular.

I submit that there are three major types of situations which give rise to individuals making unethical choices and decisions thereby causing themselves and others to engage in unethical conduct. First is the inability to recognize the existence of ethical questions in a particular situation. While some of us lie anyway, I believe virtually all of us would agree that it is wrong and we know a lie when we encounter one. Other situations are more subtle. Is it unethical to continue to follow the custom and practice of the industry when a safer method is available at comparable cost? At a greater cost? How much greater?

The second type of situation is that in which individuals must wrestle with competing pressures and responsibilities. This can run the gamut from loyalty to one's profession and employer, to the need to earn a living to support a family. How can one reconcile these competing factors?

The third type of situation is not really a "situation," but, as far as I can tell, is a factor which is a function of the human condition. (Please note here that I did not say "human nature." While I

am convinced that what I am about to say is true, I am not convinced of its origin.) This third factor is the tendency of most people to be obedient. Now, what I mean by this requires a journey
back to Psychology 100 and the work of Stanley Milgram. Stanley
Milgram is a social psychologist who set out to answer the question: "If Hitler asked you to electrocute a stranger, would you?"
His thesis was that there was something peculiar about Germans
which allowed Hitler to advance his master plan of systematically
exterminating Jews and other groups which were anathema to his
vision of a pure Aryan race. To prove his thesis, he designed a scientific study. His intent was to first show that Americans would
never engage in Nazi-like behavior. After proving Americans did
not fit the Nazi paradigm, he then intended to proceed to other
countries. Essentially, he believed his original thesis would be
proven by showing that citizens of other countries would not do
these things; hence, there was something peculiar to German cul-
ture which permitted the Nazi atrocities. Milgram started his study
in New Haven (he was on the faculty of Yale University at the
time). When his thesis was not supported, he tried Bridgeport. In
the final analysis, he never got out of Connecticut.

The experiment was staged. That is, everyone but the person
being studied (the volunteer) was acting a role. The volunteer was
assigned the role of a teacher who was to give the "student" pro-
gressively higher electrical shocks as the "student" gave incorrect
answers to questions. The shock generator had a meter which
ranged from 15 to 450 volts. Each wrong answer increased the
voltage punishment by 15 volts. In addition, the meter had labels
indicating that 15 volts was a "Slight Shock" and that at 450 volts,
the shock was classified as "Danger: Severe Shock." Even with the
"students" protesting and, in some instances, screaming as the
shocks increased, 65% of the New Haven volunteers continued to
administer the shocks to the highest level. In Bridgeport, 48% proceeded to the highest level.[17]

With these results far from supporting his original thesis, Mil-

---

[17]Manning, George and Curtis, Kent, *Ethics at Work: Fire in a Dark World*, Cincinnati: South-Western Publishing Co., 1988, p. 138.

gram sought an explanation. In his own words, he explains the results: "...they are somehow engaged in something from which they cannot liberate themselves. They are locked into a structure and they do not have the skills or inner resources to disengage themselves."[18] His final conclusion was that many people resolve conflict in favor of obedience.

> Milgram's theory assumes that people behave in two different operating modes as different as ice and water. He does not rely on Freud or sex or toilet-training hang-ups in this theory. All he says is that ordinarily we operate in a state of autonomy, which means we pretty much have and assert control over what we do. But in certain circumstances, we operate under what Milgram calls a state of agency (...one who acts for or in the place of another by authority from him: a substitute; a deputy...). A state of agency, to Milgram, is nothing more than a frame of mind.

> 'There's nothing bad about it, there's nothing good about it,' he says. 'It's a natural circumstance of living with other people...I think of a state of agency as a real transformation of a person; if a person has different properties when he's in that state, just as water can turn to ice under certain conditions of temperature, a person can move to the state of mind that I call agency...the critical thing is that you see yourself as the instrument of the execution of another person's wishes. You do not see yourself as acting on your own. And there's real transformation, a real change of properties of the person.'

> To achieve this change, you have to be in a situation where there seems to be a ruling authority whose commands are relevant to some legitimate purpose; the authority's power is not unlimited.[19]

---

[18]*Ibid.*
[19]*Ibid.*, p. 142–143. Reprinted with permission.

In reading these words, there are other thoughts which come to mind—certain rules of physics, for example. Objects in motion tend to stay in motion. Objects at rest tend to stay at rest. Individuals accustomed to following the instructions of another tend to routinely comply with instructions from that other. The difficulty of disagreeing with a superior, the fear of failing loved ones, the terror of financial ruin aside, is it possible that many ethical lapses occur simply because all of us are accustomed to the routine of following orders whether articulated or assumed? I believe the answer is a solid "yes." This is not said as a condemnation of the human race; it is an observation of the overwhelming obstacles many individuals face when confronted with actual or potential ethical dilemmas. It may be simple to state the problem, but it is not simple to solve.

Nevertheless, there is guidance to be found in the work of some who grapple with the practical nuances and difficulties of deceivingly simple propositions. One such individual is Kenneth D. Alpern who offers his prescription for improving the ethical conduct of engineers in his essay, "Moral Responsibility for Engineers."[20] Alpern offers two simple principles which can be applied to all engineering undertakings. The first is the *Principle of Care:* "Other things being equal, one should exercise due care to avoid contributing to significantly harming others." Alpern goes on to develop a companion principle which he entitles the *Corollary of Proportionate Care:* "When one is in a position to contribute to greater harm or when one is in a position to play a more critical part in producing harm than is another person, one must exercise greater care to avoid so doing." I would add a third principle to Alpern's list, the *Principle of Most Correctable Damage:* when one must select from alternatives, all of which involve potential damage, all else being equal, one should err on the side of an alterative whose damage, if it occurs, is most subject to correction. In other words, start with the alternative which can be fixed if it does not

---

[20]Alpern, Kenneth D., "Moral Responsibilities for Engineers," *Business and Professional Ethics Journal,* Vol. 2, No. 2, 1983, pp. 39–48.

work. Do not start with the alternative from which recovery from damage is not possible or is the most difficult.

Why go to the trouble in the face of so many difficulties? The answers are many. First, there are some things which should be done simply because they are right, and others which should not be done simply because they are wrong. Many of us were raised to understand that, but we have forgotten or given up on it. Second, no one of us has impeccable standing to point a finger at others if we do not keep our own houses clean. One of the dangers in, for example, cheating only a little, or ignoring it just this time, is that we become implicit co-conspirators—next time comes a little easier, or if it does not, we are more likely to be reminded that we are no paradigms of virtue ourselves. "What's wrong this time?" "You didn't have a problem when..., so get off your soapbox." Finally, in my opinion, the best reason to do the right thing against all the odds is the selfish reason. I have yet to meet an unethical person who is also a happy, healthy person. Now I admit I have drawn this conclusion without the benefit of any scientific survey. But I ask you to look around. Would you want to have to live in the skin and shoes of the unethical people you have encountered in your life? I doubt it. Do the right thing for the best of all possible reasons—to feel good about yourself.

Appendices

The following tables provide various statistics on product liability lawsuits and related matters. Please note that these statistics relate to verdicts only. That is, these data relate only to those cases which go to trial and end with a verdict entered by the court. The majority of cases do *not* go to trial. While some are withdrawn or dismissed, most cases are settled before or during the course of a trial. The following statistics *do not* reflect the outcomes of the cases which are resolved by a settlement reached by the parties.

Plaintiff Recovery Probabilities in Personal Injury Law Suits

(Product Liability Lawsuits)

	1970	1975	1980	1985	1990
Consumer	54%	51%	50%	49%	48%
Food and Beverage	66%	64%	62%	62%	51%
Industrial/Commercial	62%	60%	56%	54%	59%
Medical Products	76%	74%	74%	74%	61%
Transportation	61%	60%	57%	57%	58%

Source: Jury Verdict Research: Current Liability Trends in Personal Injury (1992).

Plaintiff Recovery By State for all Personal Injuries

(National Norm = 63%)

State	Recovery	State	Recovery
Alabama	57%	Missouri	58%
Alaska	70%	Montana	63%
Arizona	62%	Nebraska	62%
Arkansas	57%	Nevada	64%
California	64%	New Hampshire	66%
Colorado	60%	New Jersey	69%
Connecticut	67%	New Mexico	62%
Delaware	68%	New York	69%
D.C.	70%	North Carolina	60%
Florida	66%	North Dakota	62%
Georgia	57%	Ohio	64%
Hawaii	66%	Oklahoma	62%
Idaho	62%	Oregon	58%
Illinois	64%	Pennsylvania	65%
Indiana	64%	Rhode Island	62%
Iowa	62%	South Carolina	60%
Kansas	62%	South Dakota	60%
Kentucky	60%	Tennessee	62%
Louisiana	62%	Texas	64%
Maine	64%	Utah	62%
Maryland	68%	Vermont	62%
Massachusetts	70%	Virginia	65%
Michigan	66%	Washington	62%
Minnesota	65%	West Virginia	60%
Mississippi	58%	Wisconsin	62%
		Wyoming	60%

Source: Jury Verdict Research: Current Liability Trends in Personal Injury, 1990.

Product Liability Verdicts
Distribution of Verdicts

Verdict Range	Percent of Total
To 9,999	5%
$10,000–49,999	14%
$50,000–99,999	6%
$100,000–499,999	31%
$500,000–999,999	15%
$1,000,000 +	29%

Source: Jury Verdict Research: Current
Liability Trends in Personal Injury, 1990.

Million-Dollar Verdicts Reported by Liability

This table outlines the count and rank order of 18 categories of nonvehicular liabilities from 1962 to 1991

Category	Total	Rank Order
Aircraft	151	9
Bad Faith	101	11
Dramshop	41	15
False Arrest	40	16
Government Negligence	361	5
Intentional Tort	177	8
Libel and Slander	61	13
Medical Malpractice	1,032	1
Negligent Supervision	38	17
Premises and Occupier	342	6
Products Liability	**1,013**	**2**
Professional Negligence	582	3
Railroad	211	7
Shipping	49	14
Sports	29	18
Utilities	103	10
Work Related	539	4
Wrongful Termination	74	12

Source: Jury Verdict Research: Current Liability Trends in Personal Injury
(1992).

Million-Dollar Verdicts Reported by State
Personal Injury Verdicts 1962–1991

(1991 Data Is Incomplete)

State	Count	Rank Order
Alabama	89	13
Alaska	19	38
Arizona	85	14
Arkansas	36	30
California	719	2
Colorado	50	23
Connecticut	27	41
Delaware	15	40
D.C.	60	18
Florida	577	3
Georgia	93	12
Hawaii	29	34
Idaho	10	46
Illinois	259	5
Indiana	44	26
Iowa	34	32
Kansas	45	25
Kentucky	53	22
Louisiana	68	16
Maine	9	47
Maryland	50	23
Massachusetts	107	11
Michigan	251	6
Minnesota	61	17
Mississippi	26	35
Missouri	170	8
Montana	14	42
Nebraska	13	43
Nevada	26	35
New Hampshire	9	47
New Jersey	121	10
New Mexico	23	37
New York	890	1
North Carolina	39	29
North Dakota	12	44

State	Count	Rank Order
Ohio	137	9
Oklahoma	55	21
Oregon	40	28
Pennsylvania	208	7
Rhode Island	15	40
South Carolina	18	39
South Dakota	7	50
Tennessee	36	30
Texas	413	4
Utah	12	44
Vermont	2	51
Virginia	59	19
Washington	74	15
West Virginia	30	33
Wisconsin	59	19
Wyoming	8	49
TOTAL	5,320	

Three States Reported 41% of all Awards

State	Total	% (of 5,320)
New York	890	16.7%
California	719	13.5%
Florida	577	10.8%

Source: Jury Verdict Research: Current Liability Trends in Personal Injury, (1992).

Permission to reprint the preceeding tables has been granted by the publisher Jury Verdict Research, LRP Publications, 747 Dresher Road, P.O. Box 980, Horsham, PA 19044. For more information on Jury Verdict Research or any other jury verdict published by LRP Publications, please call 800-341-7874.

Verdicts by Litigant Status

(Derived from Study of State Court Cases)

Status	Plaintiff	Defendant	Total
Individual v. Individual	60.8%	39.2%	100%
Individual v. Insurance Co.	62.5%	37.5%	100%
Individual v. Corporation	50.3%	49.7%	100%
Individual v. Government	40.3%	59.7%	100%
Individual v. Individual and Corporation	51.5%	48.5%	100%
Non-individual v. Individual	78.3%	21.7%	100%
Non-individual v. Non-individual	69.0%	31.0%	100%
All Torts	56.6%	43.4%	100%

Source: Rottman, Ostrom, and Hanson, "What are Tort Awards Really Like? The Untold Story From the State Courts," 1989. Reprinted with permission from the National Center for State Courts, Williamsburg, VA.

Glossary

absolute liability: Responsibility for an injury or damage regardless of whether it was caused innocently or through negligence or fault. Synonymous with strict liability (see strict liability in tort).

assumption of the risk: A defense to a damage action. Elements: (a) the injured person knew of and appreciated the danger—there was an understanding of the risks; and (b) the injured person voluntarily chose to be exposed to the danger.

breach: The breaking or violation of an obligation or a law.

civil action: An action to enforce private rights. A lawsuit involving either (a) one private party suing another private party, or (b) a private party suing or being sued by the government, which does not directly involve criminal proceedings.

comparative negligence: 1. The measurement of negligence by percentage. 2. The damages shall be diminished in proportion to the amount of negligence attributable to the victim. 3. The victim's damages are reduced proportionately, provided his or her fault was less than that of the defendant.

contract: A legally binding agreement that creates an obligation to do or not to do a particular thing. There must be mutuality of agreement and obligation, legal consideration, and competent parties.

contributory negligence: An unreasonable act or omission on the part of the complaining party which, concurring with the defendant's negligence, is the proximate cause of the injury.

crime: A positive or negative act that violates the penal law of the State or Federal government; any act done in violation of those duties which an individual owes to the community and for the breach of which the law has decided that the offender shall make satisfaction to the public.

damages: Monetary compensation that may be recovered in court by someone who has suffered injury or loss to person, to property, or to rights through an unlawful act or omission of another.

deceit: See fraud and misrepresentation.

defective: Lacking in some particular that is essential to completeness, safety, or legal sufficiency.

defendant: The person defending or denying; the person against whom relief or recovery is sought. Respondent, accused, the party charged, the party sued, responding litigant.

defense: Allegation of fact or legal theories offered to offset or defeat claims or demands. A rebuttal.

disclaimer: The repudiation of a claim, power, or obligation.

express warranty: An affirmation of fact or promise made by the seller to the buyer, which relates to the goods and becomes part of the basis of the bargain and creates an express warranty that the goods shall conform to the affirmation. Any description of the goods and any sample or model that is made part of the basis of the bargain creates an express warranty that all of the goods shall conform to the description, sample, or model.

foreseeability: The ability to see or know in advance; the extent to which something can be known in advance; reasonable anticipation of something.

fraud: A harmfully false and deceptive statement of fact. Elements of this tort (also called deceit): (a) a statement of past or present fact, or a concealment of past or present fact, or a nondisclosure of past or present fact where there is a duty to disclose; (b) the statement is false; (c) scienter, i.e., the intent to deceive—in some States, this element is met by negligently misleading the victim; (d) the defendant intends to have the victim rely on the statement or has reason to believe that the victim will rely on it; (e) the victim actually relies on it; (f) the victim's reliance is justifiable; (g) the victim suffers actual damages. (See misrepresentation.)

implied warranty: A warranty imposed by operation of law regardless of the intent of the parties; a warranty that is based on the apparent intentions of the parties. (See warranty of fitness for a particular purpose and warranty of merchantability.)

joint and several liability: The liability that exists when a creditor or plaintiff has the option of suing one liable party separately or all liable parties together. Each wrongdoer is individually responsible for the entire judgment, and the person who has been wronged can collect from one wrongdoer or from all of them together until the judgment is satisfied.

joint tortfeasors: Two or more persons who are jointly and severally liable in tort for the same injury to person or property; persons who have acted in concert in committing a tort.

judgment: The official decision of a court in a case brought before it; a judicial determination of the rights and duties of parties growing out of litigation before a court.

law: A rule of action or conduct prescribed by a controlling authority and having binding force; that which must be obeyed.

merchantable: Fit for the ordinary purposes for which the goods are used; acceptable without objection in the trade under the contract description; conformable to ordinary standards of care; of average grade, quality, and value of similar goods sold under similar circumstances.

misrepresentation: An intentionally false statement of fact. (See fraud.)

negligence: The failure to do what a reasonable person would have done under the same circumstances. A departure of the conduct that would be expected of a reasonably prudent person under the same circumstances. A tort with the following elements: (a) a duty of reasonable care owed to the injured person, (b) a breach of this duty, (c) proximate cause, (d) actual damages.

plaintiff: The person who complains and brings an action. Complainant, claimant, appellant.

procedural law: A law that prescribes a method of enforcing rights or obtaining redress for the invasion of rights.

product liability: The liability of a manufacturer, supplier, wholesaler, assembler, retail seller, or lessor of a defective product placed on the market, which causes damage or injury. Several causes of action can be used to impose such liability: negligence, strict liability in tort, deceit, breach of express warranty, breach of implied warranty of merchantability, breach of implied warranty of fitness for a particular purpose.

punitive damages (also called exemplary damages): Having the characteristic of punishment or a penalty. Increased damages awarded to the plaintiff over and above what will compensate for his or her loss, where the wrong was aggravated by circumstances of violence, oppression, malice, fraud, or wanton conduct of the defendant.

reasonable care: The degree of care which a person of ordinary prudence would exercise in the same or similar circumstances; due care under the circumstances.

strict liability in tort: Elements of this tort: (a) a seller or person engaged in the business of selling products for use or consumption; (b) a defective product that is unreasonably dangerous to person or property, (c) causes, (d) harm, (e) to a user or consumer. Some courts have extended the last element to include bystanders.

substantive law: Law that creates, defines, and regulates rights, as opposed to adjective, procedural, or remedial law that provides a method of enforcing rights.

tort: A civil (as opposed to criminal) wrong (other than a breach of contract) that has caused harm to person or property.

verdict: The formal decision or finding of a jury, reported to the court.

warranty: A pledge that a proposition of fact is true. A guarantee.

warranty of fitness for a particular purpose: If the seller at the time of contracting has reason to know any particular purpose for which the goods are required, and the buyer is relying on the seller's skill or judgment to select or furnish goods that are suitable, there is, unless excluded or modified, an implied warranty that the goods shall be good for that purpose.

warranty of merchantability: An implied promise that the goods are reasonably fit for the general purpose for which they were sold. (See merchantable.)

Bibliography

Alpern, Kenneth D., "Moral Responsibilities for Engineers," *Business and Professional Ethics Journal,* Vol. 2, No. 2, 1983.

Averbach, Albert, *Handling Accident Cases: Products Liability,* Rochester: Lawyers Co-operative Publishing Co., 1971 (updated to 1990).

Brown, Sam (Ed.), *The Product Liability Handbook: Prevention, Risk, Consequence, and Forensics of Product Failure,* New York: Van Nostrand Reinhold, 1991.

Hall, Gerald, *The Failure to Warn Handbook,* Columbia, MD: Hanrow Press, Inc, 1986.

Henderson, James A., Jr., and Eisenberg, Theodore, "The Quiet Revolution In Products Liability: An Empirical Study of Legal Change," *37 U.C.L.A. Law Review 479,* Feb. 1990.

Hermann, Gary D., "The Consumer Expectation Test Application of a Difficult Standard for Determining Product Defects," *41 Federation of Insurance and Corporate Counsel Quarterly 251,* Winter 1991.

Johnson, Deborah G., *Ethical Issues in Engineering,* Englewood Cliffs, NJ: Prentice-Hall, Inc., 1991.

Johnson, Tami I., "Limiting Manufacturers' Liability for Aging Products," *39 Drake Law Review 713,* 1989–1990.

Jury Verdict Research: Current Award Trends in Personal Injury, Vol. 1, Solon OH: Jury Verdict Research Inc., 1990.

Jury Verdict Research, Current Liability Trends in Personal Injury, Vol. 1, Solon, OH: Jury Verdict Research Inc., 1990 and 1992 Eds.

Jury Verdict Research: Injury Valuation, Vol 2, Solon, OH: Jury Verdict Research Inc., 1990.

Kiely, Terrence F., *Preparing Products Liability Cases,* New York: John Wiley & Sons, 1986.

Manning, George and Curtis, Kent, *Ethics at Work: Fire in a Dark World,* Cincinnati, OH: South-Western Publishing Co., 1988.

Morton, Rebecca, *Engineering Law, Design Liability, and Professional Ethics: An Introduction for Engineers,* San Carlos, CA: Professional Publications, Inc., 1983.

Mundel, August B., *Ethics in Quality,* New York: ASQC Quality Press, 1991.

Products Liability Basics, Boston, MA: Massachusetts Continuing Legal Education, Inc., 1990.

Product Liability for the Sophisticated Practitioner, Boston, MA: Massachusetts Continuing Legal Education, 1989.

Prosser, William L., *Handbook of the Law of Torts, 4th ed.,* St. Paul, MN: West Publishing Co., 1971.

Rottman, David B.; Ostrom, Brian J.; and Hanson, Roger, "What Are Tort Awards Really Like? The Untold Story From the State Courts," Williamsburg, VA: National Center for State Courts, 1989.

Schaub, James H. and Pavlovic, Karl, *Engineering Professionalism and Ethics,* Malabar, FL: Robert E. Krieger Publishing Co., 1986.

Spencer, William H., *A Textbook of Law and Business,* New York: McGraw-Hill Book Company, Inc., 1938.

Unger, Stephen H., *Controlling Technology: Ethics and the Responsible Engineer,* New York: CBS College Publishing, 1982.

Weinstein, Aven; Twerski, Aaron D.; Piehler, Henry R.; and Donaher, William A., *Products Liability and the Reasonably Safe Product,* New York: John Wiley & Sons, 1978.

White, James J. and White, Robert S., *Handbook of the Law Under the Uniform Commercial Code,* St. Paul, MN: West Publishing Company, 1972.

Index of Cited Cases

Index

Definition, 113
Legal risks, 108

Manufacturing defects, 2, 9, 13,
    30–32, 35–38, 51
Merchantable
    Definition, 130
    See implied warranty of mer-
        chantability
Misrepresentation, 2, 4, 8, 9, 38,
    40, 41, 50, 51, 61
    Definition, 130
    See fraud
Mistrial, 96

Negligence, 8, 10, 11, 13–15, 17–
    19, 22–25, 28–31, 33–35, 37,
    41, 69, 70, 74–89, 92, 99, 100
    Definition, 130

Obedient behavior, 117–119
    See ethics
Objections, 96, 97
Opening statements, 96

Plaintiff, 93, 94
    Definition, 130
Principal of care, 119
    See ethics
Principal of most correctable dam-
    age, 119
    See ethics
Procedural law, 5, 93
    Definition, 130
Product liability, 1, 4, 7–10, 14, 50,
    62, 71
Product liability loss assurance
    committee, 57, 60
Product misuse, 2
    See contributory negligence,
        comparative negligence, and
        assumption of the risk
Products, 109, 115
Product redesign, 109
Profession(al), 10, 114
    Judgment, 108
    See engineer

Proof, 102
    See evidence
Puffing, 39, 41, 44, 49
    See sales talk and warranty
Punitive damages
    Definition, 130

Quality assurance, 55, 57, 58, 61

Reasonable care, 12, 23, 28, 34
    Definition, 131
    See negligence
Recall programs, 31, 110
Recklessness, 116
Record retention policy, 110
Repair records, 95, 110
    See customers and consumer
        complaints
Requests for the production of
    documents, 95

Safety standards, 21, 23, 52, 53, 58
Sales talk
    See puffing
Spoilation of evidence, 110
State-of-the-art defense, 73, 86, 87,
    90–92
Stipulations, 94
Strict liability, 8, 10, 13, 14, 16–20,
    22, 23, 30, 31, 37, 38, 66, 69,
    83, 86, 88–90, 92
    See absolute liability
Strict liability in tort
    Definition, 131
    See strict liability and absolute
        liability
Substantive law, 5, 93
    Definition, 131

Tables
    Distribution of product liability
        verdicts, 123
    Million dollor verdicts reported
        by liability, 123
    Million dollar verdicts reported
        by state, 124–125
    Plaintiff recovery by state for